BECKY SHAW

BY GINA GIONFRIDDO

DRAMATISTS
PLAY SERVICE
INC.

2

For Adrien-Alice Hansel

AUTHOR'S NOTE

I want to share a few beliefs about this play that I hope will function as permissions rather than prescriptions.

I don't think any character in this play is bad or wrong or crazy or worthless or unlovable. I don't think any of them are damaged beyond repair. I don't think any one character is more to blame than the others for the emotional wreckage that piles up in the second act.

I wish fingers didn't have to be pointed, but — trust me — they will be. In the audience talkbacks I have taken part in after productions of *Becky Shaw*, the one constant I have seen is the zeal to ascribe blame. The good news is that the audiences invariably fail to reach consensus as to which character is most deserving of their contempt. These characters seem to function as screens onto which audience members project old wounds and fierce convictions about how people ought to behave. The best comment I ever got in one of these talkbacks was from a woman who shook her head wistfully at the people arguing around her and opined that the characters were all "just doing the best they can."

And I agree. There isn't any character in this play I wouldn't fix up with one of my friends. With some caveats, of course. I might say, "I have this great person in mind, but here's a thing or two you should know ..." But I would say this about any of my actual real friends in my actual real life. Like Suzanna says, "First date, everyone's nervous ... We all have our thing." I'm not convinced these characters have significantly more things than your average Janes and Joes.

For whatever reason, I have seen Becky and Andrew take some of the harder beatings in these discussions, so I want to speak specifically to them. In imagining Becky, think of the fallen stars you've known, the people who came out of high school voted most likely to succeed and ... didn't. At seventeen, Becky had looks, brains, charm, and a full scholarship to an Ivy League school. Now she is, as Max rightly points out, "a thirty-five-year-old office temp" with a barren personal life. How did that happen? I think it happened for the reasons Becky gives in the play, and for a few others she doesn't give. I leave the specifics of Becky's slide to the actress who plays her. The point I wish to drive home is that Becky is not a psycho loser but rather a winner who skidded off course and, through accumulated disappointments and failures, lost her moorings.

I have respect for Becky, and I have hope. She has an iron will not to accept her fate — her thin paycheck and monotonous typing-pool poverty. I believe that the woman Max describes at the end of the café scene — bitter, desperate, mercenary — is someone Becky truly does not want to be. It's fine to feel frustrated by Becky, oppressed by her, angry with her. Just keep in mind that she feels these same things about herself. Do I think Max and Becky have a future together? I don't know. But I don't think it's out of the question. If Becky were to work very hard and reclaim that old, good self she alludes to in the café ... Who knows?

Some words on Andrew. The potential pitfall in playing this character is to play the purity and truth of his goodness. I'm not sure I believe anyone is totally good and true, and I certainly don't believe Andrew is. If he seems more straightforward than the other characters, it may be because he's operating under the most self-delusion. He's a serial rescuer who derives self-esteem and maybe even sexual arousal from assuming the savior role in women's lives. He's got a bit of a broken bird fetish. Is this a terrible, wicked thing? I don't think it is. Suzanna isn't wrong to credit Andrew with "healing her." I think every character in this play manipulates other people to get their own needs met, and Andrew is no exception. He will come to understand this about himself in the course of the play, and it's an uncomfortable truth to face. I think the play works best when the actor playing Andrew mines the darker impulses in this very nice guy's character.

A couple more things that may help ...

I've heard from some of the artists who've worked on the play that they enjoyed knowing what I was chewing on when I sat down to write *Becky Shaw*. I was reading Thackeray's novel *Vanity Fair* after being intrigued by comments the film director, Mira Nair, made regarding the perils of adapting the book for film in 1994. Also, I was puzzling over the many novels I read in college named after female characters that are (a) destroyers, (b) victims of destruction, or (c) both. Most often, they are both; their terrible reversals wrought by sexual indiscretions and attempts to climb into a higher class. I'm thinking of novels from the 18th, 19th, and early 20th centuries, mostly — books by Richardson, Flaubert, Tolstoy, Hardy, and Dreiser, to name a few. On the dramatic front, I'd throw in *Hedda Gabler* and *Miss Julie*. I tried to change the name of this play at one point and my director, Peter DuBois, urged me not to do it. He said that the title *Becky Shaw* felt ominous and perilous for reasons he could not name. He led me to understand that we have a great literary tradition of ruinous and ruined eponymous women that we've internalized without analyzing.

Lastly, I know I have misquoted *Nightmare on Elm Street 3: Dream Warriors*. Over their years of friendship, Max and Suzanna have misremembered the quotation and — I think — slightly improved upon the original text. If it trips you up, you can change Max's line to "Bitch, where's the fucking bourbon?" But don't change Suzanna's.

I want to thank a few people not credited elsewhere who were in the development trenches with me and helped me find the play I wanted to write: Arija Bareikis, Patch Darragh, Dashiell Eaves, Morgan Hallett, Charles Haugland, Jesse Hooker, and Zan Sawyer-Daily.

Thanks for hearing me out. Have fun.

Gina Gionfriddo
February 2010

BECKY SHAW was commissioned by Actors Theatre of Louisville (Marc Masterson, Artistic Director) and had its world premiere at the Humana Festival of New American Plays in February 2008. It was directed by Peter DuBois; the set design was by Paul Owen; the lighting design was by Brian J. Lilienthal; the sound design was by Benjamin Marcum; the costume design was by Jessica Ford; the dramaturg was Adrien-Alice Hansel; and the stage manager was Michael D. Domue. The cast was as follows:

MAX GARRETT .... David Wilson Barnes
SUZANNA SLATER .... Mia Barron
SUSAN SLATER .... Janis Dardaris
BECKY SHAW .... Annie Parisse
ANDREW PORTER .... Davis Duffield

BECKY SHAW premiered Off-Broadway at Second Stage Theatre (Carole Rothman, Artistic Director), opening January 8, 2009. It was directed by Peter DuBois; the set design was by Derek McLane; the costume design was by Jeff Mahshie; the lighting design was by David Weiner; the sound design was by Walter Trarbach; and the production stage manager was Lori Ann Zepp. The cast was as follows:

MAX GARRETT .... David Wilson Barnes
SUZANNA SLATER .... Emily Bergl
SUSAN SLATER .... Kelly Bishop
BECKY SHAW .... Annie Parisse
ANDREW PORTER .... Thomas Sadoski

CHARACTERS

MAX GARRETT

SUZANNA SLATER

SUSAN SLATER

BECKY SHAW

ANDREW PORTER

PLACE AND TIME

The United States (New York City, Providence, and Boston), 2009.

BECKY SHAW

ACT ONE

Scene 1

A room at a mid-range hotel in New York City. Suzanna, thirty-four, sits on the (made) bed, watching a Forensic Files*–like true crime program on TV. She's wearing a black dress (plain and casual; nothing sexy, formal, or funereal). She's cozied-up and mesmerized ... soothed by a story of female disaster worse than her own. The narrator reports on a dead woman in an eerie monotone. Something like: "The young mother had been strangled ... and stabbed thirty-seven times." Max, thirty-five, lets himself into the room — a man on a mission, energized. He watches enough of the TV show to realize what it is, then uses the remote to turn it off.*

SUZANNA. Hey! I'm watching that.
MAX. He strangled her. She's not coming home.
SUZANNA. Turn it back on.
MAX. No. I cut you off, remember? You're not allowed to watch that stuff.
SUZANNA. It soothes me and I need it. Don't judge me.
MAX. I'm not judging you. I'm disciplining you.
SUZANNA. I did nothing wrong! My mother is the one who showed up —
MAX. Stop! I just spent forty minutes calming your mother down, and she will be here soon. You need to be a big girl and face your big girl problems. *(Indicating TV.)* No more dead prostitutes on the autopsy channel until you do that.

9

SUZANNA. Why do you have a key to my room?

MAX. Because I paid for it.

SUZANNA. Did you pay for my mom's room, too?

MAX. Yes.

SUZANNA. Because we're poor now?

MAX. That's ... what we're all gonna talk about at dinner. Your mother'll be here soon.

SUZANNA. I've decided I won't see her.

MAX. Excuse me — what?

SUZANNA. I am grieving my father's death. My mother brought a ... a man with her. To a meeting about the estate. That is so insulting to my father.

MAX. Your father's dead. His feelings don't matter.

SUZANNA. Max!

MAX. Suzanna, you made a big scene in the lobby. You made your point.

SUZANNA. I won't see her.

MAX. So ... how's this gonna work? I go to dinner with your mother and her manfriend ... You stay here and cry while she takes all the money?

SUZANNA. You would never let that happen.

MAX. You know, I might. I don't like this weepy-weepy wah-wah thing you're doing. I don't respect it.

SUZANNA. Max, I'm grieving.

MAX. Negotiations are all about who has the biggest dick in the room ... Be sad, grieve. But do it with a big dick.

SUZANNA. Grieve with a big dick? That's not possible.

MAX. Uhhh ... Charles Bronson in *Death Wish*? *Rambo*? Mrs. Voorhees in *Friday the 13th*?

SUZANNA. None of those people are real, Max!

MAX. Suzanna, you gotta pull it together. Clock strikes midnight, you can regress. Light your vanilla candle and write in your dream journal. Until then, you're a soldier. Fix yourself up.

SUZANNA. *(As she tries ...)* In one of my textbooks, I read about these families ... Craziest thing, Max. When someone in the family is in pain, the other family members do this thing called nurture. You ever heard of that?

MAX. No. *(There's a knock on the door. Max springs to answer it.)* No crying. Big dick. *(Max answers the door and escorts Susan Slater, sixty, into the room. She has MS and may use a cane. She's attractive, but there's a heaviness to her: the fatigue of endless fatigue. Her mind is sharp and she's cultivated a forceful manner to compensate for her physical disability.)* OK. So. Clean slate. Last few hour's never happened. I'd like to welcome my two favorite ladies to New York City. We're all so glad we're here because we love each other so much, etc., etc. Now. I'm gonna suggest that we stick to the original plan.

SUSAN. I never suggested otherwise.

SUZANNA. You brought Lester! The plan did not include Lester!

SUSAN. Suzanna, I am disabled. I can't travel alone.

SUZANNA. I offered to drive to Richmond and pick you up —

SUSAN. I don't feel safe in a car with you. I'm sorry if that hurts your feelings, but —

MAX. It hurts my feelings, Susan. I taught her to drive.

SUSAN. I'm not blaming you. Suzanna has assumed a somber attitude since her father died.

SUZANNA. So I can't drive?

SUSAN. You're sluggish. If a drunk driver is careening into my path, I don't want my life in your hands. I'm sorry.

MAX. Suzanna's attitude is not the point. Lester is not the point.

SUZANNA. Lester is the point! I am not going to discuss my father's estate with your ... whatever he is to you in addition to being your house painter ...

SUSAN. He's my lover.

SUZANNA. Oh, my God. How could you?

SUSAN. *(Anger spikes.)* Listen to me. Your father died six months ago ...

SUZANNA. It was three months!

MAX. Four. It was four months; you're both liars.

SUSAN. You didn't lose a child or even a breast. Your father died of natural causes after a life well-lived. That's not loss, it's transition.

SUZANNA. How can you ... It's a huge loss.

SUSAN. It's an old man dying peacefully. It's not tragic —

SUZANNA. He was my dad.

SUSAN. And you're an adult. This ... This is a costume.

SUZANNA. What — my clothes?

SUSAN. The black dress. You're infatuated with your grief. You think you've finally found something that will distinguish you.

MAX. OK, that's enough.

SUSAN. It's not a distinction, Suzanna. A parent's death ... It is the most common of milestones —

MAX. My proposal is that we keep to the plan. We go to dinner, we talk facts and figures. Lester can join us for dessert.

SUSAN. No. I won't leave him sitting in the room while we have our nice dinner.

MAX. See ... *This* is the point. It's not going to be a nice dinner, Susan. We're here to talk about your finances —

SUSAN. I don't discuss money at the dinner table. You grew up in my household; you know that.

MAX. Oh, no. No. You agreed to this!

SUSAN. I agreed to hear your opinions —

MAX. They're not opinions.

SUSAN. I'm perfectly willing to have a conversation about the estate, but not over dinner. *(To Suzanna.)* Some women — Marilyn Monroe, Princess Diana — are sensual in grief. You are not.

SUZANNA. Max!

MAX. Susan, please —

SUSAN. Do you disagree? Look at her.

MAX. Let me tell you something. Suzanna can be fixed. I'm not worried about Suzanna. Your financial health, on the other hand —

SUSAN. Lester and I will meet you downstairs. We'll share a meal and some good wine. We'll talk business in the morning.

MAX. No! I don't have time in the morning, Susan! And you can't afford good wine.

SUSAN. *(After a beat.)* Are you enjoying this drama you've created?

MAX. Your husband created it. I am just the messenger.

SUSAN. This is terribly exhilarating for you. I can see it.

SUZANNA. Mom.

MAX. How can you ... You and Richard raised me, Susan. For all practical purposes, you're my parents.

SUSAN. And that only makes it crueler.

MAX. You think I take pleasure in this? I would be a monster —

SUSAN. Not a monster, a powermonger. I know that look.

MAX. What look? This look?

SUSAN. That is the look you get when my family's stupidity offers you a foothold to gain power.

MAX. Anytime I can clean up after your family's stupidity, I'm happy to do it.

SUZANNA. Stop it. What is this "your family," "my family." We're ... This is our family. *(A difficult silence that Suzanna rushes to fill ...)* How broke are we?

MAX. I think we should drink some alcohol.

SUSAN. Lester is hungry. Whatever you want to say, you may say now or in the morning.

MAX. I have a full day tomorrow —

SUSAN. Then say it now. Cogently, please. Do not savor.

MAX. *(After a beat.)* The business hasn't turned a profit in nearly a decade. Richard burned through a lot of your savings patching holes, keeping it afloat. I think it was largely ... sentimental. It's an old family business, he hoped the tide would turn ...

SUZANNA. Are we broke?

MAX. No. But your savings are ... thin. I have a plan I would like to propose —

SUSAN. I have a very hard time believing this, Max. Yoshi would certainly have told me if —

MAX. Yoshi lost his objectivity. He'll be the first to admit that ...

SUSAN. Nonsense. He's a Japanese businessman. His objectivity is all he has.

SUZANNA. Mom, that's racist.

SUSAN. Send me the figures, I will show them to my financial advisor.

MAX. Your financial advisor is Yoshi.

SUSAN. Correct.

MAX. Yoshi no longer wishes to be involved.

SUSAN. Because you bullied him in your zeal to seize power. I'll bring him back.

MAX. There's no power to seize, Susan! *(Pause.)* Look. Yoshi asked me ... There was a loss of objectivity.

SUSAN. In your opinion ...

MAX. In reality on planet Earth. Your husband was stupid about his money and his financial advisor was ... There was a romantic situation and I'm sorry.

SUSAN. *(After a beat.)* Oh, you are devious.

SUZANNA. Romantic?

SUSAN. He means homosexual.

MAX. I don't think we need to get into labels.

SUZANNA. Gay?

MAX. Bi. Let's say your father was bi.

SUZANNA. You don't believe in bisexuality.

SUSAN. I'm very upset with you, Max.

MAX. Me?

SUSAN. *(Rising to leave.)* Lester and I will be having dinner privately and returning to Richmond.

MAX. Susan, you gotta face this.

SUSAN. *(To Max.)* I hope you enjoyed yourself. You could have done this in an email, as I begged you to do. *(To Suzanna.)* You're welcome to join us for dinner if you're prepared to apologize to Lester for your dramatics.

SUZANNA. Mom, you need to stay with me and deal with this. *(Susan looks back and forth ... at Max, at Suzanna. Her gaze lands on Max.)*

SUSAN. No good deed goes unpunished. You ... were a good deed.

MAX. I know that.

SUSAN. I took you into my home ...

SUZANNA. Mom. Stop.

MAX. You did. I owe your family a debt and I'm ready to start repaying it tonight. Let me help you — *(Susan makes a dismissive swipe at the air and starts walking to the door ...)* I manage money for a living, Susan. I make people rich. You could do worse than having me —

SUSAN. You ... You are a rich man ... who puts his family in a two-star hotel. That's what you are. *(Susan leaves, closing the door hard behind her.)*

MAX. You're going to have to hire someone else to do this. There's too much history — *(After a beat.)* This is a three-star hotel.

SUZANNA. Max, I'm sorry.

MAX. I think the MS is catching up to her. Since when does she run from a shitstorm?

SUZANNA. She likes other people's shitstorms. This is too close.

MAX. Is that it? *(After a beat.)* You know ... The day of my mother's funeral, she bought me a suit. I'm ten years old, I'd met her, like ... once. She took me to the fat child department at Sears. She said, "Your mother is dead and your father dresses you like a gay hustler."

SUZANNA. Max, that's awful. Why have you never told me that?

MAX. It was awful at the time, but ... She saved me from walking into my mother's funeral looking like a gay hustler. Everybody else was ... blubbering all over themselves. She's the only person who had my back. *(After a beat.)* Your dad and Yoshi ... You either knew, or you surmised. You barely reacted, and given what a fucking drama queen you are ...

14

SUZANNA. I was counting on a deathbed last scene where I would ask him.

MAX. You were saving the hard questions until he was too feeble to run?

SUZANNA. It's not like that. Did you know?

MAX. I knew there was something. A factor X that would explain him. I figured he was gay ... or impotent ... or he'd ... killed a drifter and your mother had proof, so he couldn't leave.

SUZANNA. God, I should have asked him.

MAX. He just would have denied it. He was a lying denying kinda guy.

SUZANNA. Don't say that.

MAX. He was a liar and a denier AND the greatest man I've ever known. *(Pause.)* Your parents complemented each other. Your father denied problems, your mother rubbed your face in them.

SUZANNA. He did not deny. My father had an appropriate grasp of how much a child could handle.

MAX. Right. He lied.

SUZANNA. That's what parents are supposed to do, dumbass.

MAX. Lie to children?

SUZANNA. Yes. He lied to me about my mother's illness until I was old enough to deal with it, and that was a gift.

MAX. A gift?

SUZANNA. You can't tell an eight-year-old that her mother has MS.

MAX. Susie, he told you she was an alcoholic and she wasn't.

SUZANNA. He never said "alcoholic." He said, "Sometimes Mommy drinks too much and that makes her drop things."

MAX. Well. You're going to graduate school in psychology. Get some feedback on that episode and get back to me.

SUZANNA. Max, there are times when lying is the most humane thing you can do.

MAX. I see. Your father spends his life being "humane." He leaves me to be the asshole ...

SUZANNA. I'm sorry. It's not fair to you —

MAX. No, it's fair. I owe him something. He was generous to me beyond all reason.

SUZANNA. He was generous to you because he adored you.

MAX. *(A doubting look, and then ...)* Well. When my father and I showed up at your house to say my mother had died, both of your parents said, "I'm sorry, Matt."

15

SUZANNA. They said Max. You misheard them.

MAX. It's fine. I know I was your dad's good deed. I mean … It wasn't pure charity. He thought an orphan in the house would make your mother behave better.

SUZANNA. Well, that is true, but … It didn't work, did it? She stayed evil and he kept you anyway. Because he loved you!

MAX. It was a bold move. Adopting a child to shame your wife into being less abusive … That took some balls.

SUZANNA. *(After a beat.)* Can I finish graduate school?

MAX. Yes. You're not rich anymore, but you're not the fucking Joads.

SUZANNA. So what do we do?

MAX. Sell the company. Sell the house. Your mother can get a full-service apartment. They carry the groceries, they clean. The rest of her needs … Lester can pick up the slack.

SUZANNA. Lester is the slack. He's a rentboy.

MAX. Yes, he is, and it's honest work.

SUZANNA. No, it isn't!

MAX. Lester will do everything your father did for your mother. Whatever his price, it's worth it.

SUZANNA. No.

MAX. What's your solution? You gonna move home and help her?

SUZANNA. God, no. She needs to hire someone.

MAX. The money isn't there, Suzanna. Her health is gonna decline and Lester is a decent guy …

SUZANNA. He's dumb and he's our age.

MAX. He's not dumb. He's a redneck, but he's a sort of … alternative redneck. He wants to make a movie.

SUZANNA. So that's why he's with her! Fuck that.

MAX. You want your freedom? Open your eyes. Your freedom is rentboys and redneck cinema.

SUZANNA. You're talking about prostitution.

MAX. Prostitution, marriage … Same thing. It's two people coming together because each has something the other wants.

SUZANNA. Wait. You don't believe in love?

MAX. Sure I do. Love is a happy by-product of use.

SUZANNA. *(After a beat.)* A happy by-product of use? What the fuck does that mean?

MAX. Suzanna, we're animals! Love is just … It's a feeling. Like hunger, like cold. It's a feeling that tells you what you need to survive. A sandwich, a sweater, an orphan, a … Lester.

16

SUZANNA. Stop calling yourself an orphan. Do you think all love is use or just romantic love?

MAX. All love. Your father, for example, paid our college tuition. We, in turn, loved him very much.

SUZANNA. I hate when you do this.

MAX. Do what?

SUZANNA. Turn a beautiful thing to shit!

MAX. Understanding behavior is not "turning it to shit"!

SUZANNA. You're saying my father was generous with us because he couldn't love men? Is that it?

MAX. I think if your father had been more self-actualized, I'd have college loans. I do believe that.

SUZANNA. I don't. And now I want to stop talking about this.

MAX. You're getting a Ph.D. in psychology. How are you so totally unwilling to ask the hard questions?

SUZANNA. I ask them when it's necessary. When there's no problem … It's like shoving your face in the toilet after you shit. You can do it, but it's not necessary.

MAX. Wow. You're gonna make an interesting therapist. *(After a beat.)* I'm proud of you. I just told you you're broke and you have a gay dad. And you're … I feel like I can go to bed and not worry about you.

SUZANNA. You worry about me? Since when?

MAX. Of course I worry about you. You're a mess.

SUZANNA. My father's only been dead three months.

MAX. It's four months! God. It's long enough to grieve. You have too much time on your hands —

SUZANNA. I'm in a Ph.D. program, Max!

MAX. In psychology. If you had gone to medical school like I told you to, you couldn't call me crying; you'd be too busy saving lives.

SUZANNA. Am I inconveniencing you by calling? I'll stop.

MAX. Call me all you want, I can't help you. You need to take action.

SUZANNA. I'm in therapy.

MAX. That's not action, that's wallowing.

SUZANNA. What's your idea of action?

MAX. Uh … Things you do outside your home that require you to move your limbs. You need to join some clubs …

SUZANNA. Clubs? What kind of clubs?

MAX. Clubs! The KKK, the Daughters of the American Revolution … You need activities so that when you get mopey-mopey weepy-

17

weepy, you can abort the thoughts. You can say, "I don't have time for this. I have a ... barn-raising I need to jog to."

SUZANNA. Max, cut me some slack. Dad was my anchor in the world. I feel totally untethered ...

MAX. Right. You need to fucking tether yourself. Join like a ... powder-puff, girl-on-girl softball team. Do something!

SUZANNA. I don't know. I think maybe there's value in just ... sitting with it. This feeling of floating alone in the universe. Maybe I'm supposed to learn something from it.

MAX. You've had four months. You haven't learned anything.

SUZANNA. I'm talking about life lessons, Max. It's not like learning Photoshop.

MAX. So when you call me at three A.M. saying you want to ... be dead, I should say, "Be very still, Suzanna, and reflect on your pain." That doesn't help you!

SUZANNA. It's not either/or, Max. You can offer empathy ...

MAX. You're paying a therapist for empathy and you're still calling me saying some very scary things ...

SUZANNA. They're normal impulses and they pass.

MAX. I hope so. They're hard to listen to. I need to go to bed.

SUZANNA. Now? It's so early.

MAX. I go to work at seven. I need to be in bed by ten which gives me ..., just enough time for take-out and pornography.

SUZANNA. Let's order food here.

MAX. Can we watch pornography?

SUZANNA. I don't know. I feel like our father is sort of, like, in the room ...

MAX. He wasn't "our father." I have an actual, living father who would be very hurt to hear you say that.

SUZANNA. How is he?

MAX. I don't want to talk about that.

SUZANNA. That bad, huh?

MAX. No ... It's just ... It's more complicated financial stuff.

SUZANNA. He's not gonna go to jail again, is he?

MAX. It's enough family drama for one night.

SUZANNA. Sorry. Not only do we all dump our problems on you, they're not even interesting problems. It's all ... math.

MAX. Math, I can do. A little Japanese man crying all over me in a Starbucks, I can't —

SUZANNA. Yoshi! Wow. Was he super sad?

MAX. Oh, yeah. *(After a beat.)* I want you to call your mother tomorrow and suggest that someone other than me do this. I know you're in your sad Buddhist phase, but —

SUZANNA. I will call her.

MAX. *(After a beat.)* So, let's pick some activities. Right now. Al-Anon, Unitarianism, the Green Party ... what are you gonna do?

SUZANNA. I don't know. There's a grad school ski trip. Next week.

MAX. Go.

SUZANNA. I don't ski. It's cheap, though.

MAX. Go. Go skiing. Get a dog. Kiss a girl. Shake things up.

SUZANNA. No dogs, but ... Skiing I would try.

MAX. Great. Now let's watch pornography.

SUZANNA. Remember that big ... porn superstore we used to drive past on the way to the mall? I remember the day I saw the word "amateur" on the marquee for the first time. You were driving and I said —

MAX. "Who wants to watch sexual amateurs?"

SUZANNA. I thought it meant, like, people who didn't know what they were doing.

MAX. I remember. You ever watch the amateur stuff?

SUZANNA. *(After a beat.)* A little.

MAX. OK, so you know what these "amateurs" look like.

SUZANNA. They're not all fat and ugly, Max. That's just not true.

MAX. It is true. The hot amateurs are being paid, so they're not really amateurs.

SUZANNA. Yeah, I can't watch that — girls in this country illegally and addicted to drugs ...

MAX. What consenting adults do to get into this country and stay here is not my problem.

SUZANNA. I didn't say it was. Relax.

MAX. The true amateurs are fat couples with cameras and no shame. They're disgusting. I hate them.

SUZANNA. Well, that's the only porn I can watch. All the rest ... I feel too responsible. You know?

MAX. No. *(A beat.)* See, you are why civilization is gonna end. You would choose a disgusting reality over a beautiful fiction. I don't understand that. I want *The Love Boat*. I do not want a real boat with real lovers.

SUZANNA. *The Love Boat* ... Wow. Remember ... the Saturday your mom died, we watched that on TV while my parents got your dad drunk?

MAX. Not really.

SUZANNA. We did a thousand-piece puzzle and watched *The Love Boat*.

MAX. Wait. The puzzle. Was it porpoises or something?

SUZANNA. It was a whale! I remember *The Love Boat* ending and my dad's footsteps and I thought … it's over. Max has to go home. And I prayed that wouldn't happen.

MAX. What do you mean, you prayed?

SUZANNA. I prayed. I said please God, don't let this end. I didn't pray for your mom to be alive, or my mom to be … not sick. I prayed for more time with you. And my prayer got answered. Dad came around the corner with hot chocolate. We passed out during *Fantasy Island*.

MAX. I don't remember any of that. Let's watch TV.

SUZANNA. I don't want to watch porn, though.

MAX. Fine. How about horror?

SUZANNA. Oh, yes please. Can you find some?

MAX. I can try. (*Max takes the remote, and starts channel-surfing as they get cozy on the bed. The old childhood closeness with an adult charge that scares them.*)

SUZANNA. Now I want hot chocolate. Hot chocolate and horror. That is what I want more than anything in the world.

MAX. Don't pray. Or if you do, don't squander it. Pray for money.

SUZANNA. I would never pray for money.

MAX. OK. Here. Look. *Nightmare on Elm Street*. But which one? Hundred bucks if you know.

SUZANNA. It's … Gimme a second … It's … three! Freddy's about to say, "Where's the bourbon, bitch?"

MAX. You're right. Good call! (*A beat. They watch* A Nightmare on Elm Street 3. *Then …)* "Where's the bourbon, bitch?" Like it's not bad enough he has knives for fingers; he has to be verbally abusive.

SUZANNA. I saw a rock concert at Jones Beach last year … It was late at night and freezing even though it was summer. And they didn't sell booze, so … I drank hot chocolate.

MAX. (*After a beat.*) That's it? That's the whole story.

SUZANNA. Yeah.

MAX. That's not a story. That's a set-up for a story.

SUZANNA. It's a snapshot. An exhilarating moment.

MAX. If that was exhilarating, you left a part out.

SUZANNA. I asked the concessions guy why they didn't sell booze and he said that a girl had been struck by lightning the year before. So they stopped serving booze.

MAX. *(After a beat.)* That makes absolutely no sense.

SUZANNA. The guy next to me bought a Coke and the concessions guy poured it out of the bottle into a cup. And, again, I asked why. And he said that somebody had thrown a bottle on stage the night before and hit the singer in the head. So no more bottles. *(A beat. A look. They watch the movie. Suzanna thinks ...)* OK, I got it. The point.

MAX. Fantastic.

SUZANNA. I had this moment ... this wave of exhilaration came over me and the exhilaration was feeling ... It was worth it. People getting struck by lightning and whacked in the head with bottles ... A certain amount of ... brutality was worth it to see a rock concert next to the ocean. The night your mom died felt like that, you know? My mother was sick, yours was dead ... But I felt so happy to be with you. Maybe that's how life works, you know? All these hideous things, but you get little pockets of joy to get you through. Rock concerts on the ocean. Puzzles and TV. *(Max kisses her and she lets him. She starts kissing back and stops.)* Max, I can't. You're my brother.

MAX. I'm not your brother. I think your mother hammered that point home.

SUZANNA. OK ... You're my ... money manager.

MAX. I am. Keep kissing me, I might take that responsibility seriously.

SUZANNA. I can't.

MAX. You don't want to.

SUZANNA. I really want to.

MAX. So what's the problem?

SUZANNA. It's ... epic. It's ...

MAX. It doesn't have to change anything.

SUZANNA. Really?

MAX. Really. *(Leaving the TV on, they start making out. Reluctant at first, Suzanna soon reciprocates with Max's level of enthusiasm. A sense on both sides that this was a long time coming. Lights fade ...)*

Scene 2

Eight months later. Saturday night. Andrew and Suzanna's apartment in Providence, Rhode Island. Suzanna, standing, talks on a cell phone.

SUZANNA. Hi. It's Suzanna. This is my fifth call and I'm worried … I am worried and my husband is worried. We're afraid you're dead or injured. We just … No. You know what? I know you're not dead or injured. You're just being you and thinking only of yourself. So … So fuck you, you know? Just fuck you. Fuck. You. Mom. Call me. *(Andrew, thirty-one, enters with an open laptop computer.)*
ANDREW. OK, there are no flights tonight out of Providence. Cheapest flight … out of Boston to Key West is … nine hundred seventy-five dollars. Round trip.
SUZANNA. Nine hundred? What the fuck am I supposed to do, Andrew? She's not answering her phone, we know she used her health insurance …
ANDREW. But that could mean nothing. For all you know, she has, like, a yeast infection …
SUZANNA. Yuck! Andrew, that's my mother.
ANDREW. I think if it were serious, Lester would have called.
SUZANNA. No. If it were serious, Lester would empty her bank account and flee to Mexico.
ANDREW. They've been together almost a year. I think if he was gonna kill her, he'd have done it by now.
SUZANNA. That's not how psychopaths work, stupid! They take time to gain your trust. I love that you're not a psychopath. I view this as the biggest accomplishment of my life: I married a man who is not a psychopath.
ANDREW. Well … Thank you. But don't call me stupid. And call Lester.
SUZANNA. No! I told you, Andrew. I set a boundary with my mother. She can't just act out and make me reverse myself.
ANDREW. She's not acting out. Something happened to her that required medical attention.

22

SUZANNA. Wait. You do think it's something bad. When does the flight leave?

ANDREW. Ten o'clock. How 'bout I call Lester?

SUZANNA. Fuck no. You're my husband. If I make a boundary, it's your boundary, too. *(Pause.)* Andrew, what should I do?

ANDREW. That's up to you. I will support whatever —

SUZANNA. Don't throw the decision back to me when I ask you … Sorry. I'm freaking out. I need you to tell me what to do. *(Andrew pours her a glass of wine.)*

ANDREW. First you need to drink some wine and chill.

SUZANNA. Again — That's not an answer!

ANDREW. Sweetie, I can't be your dad. You're gonna have to participate in the decision.

SUZANNA. What's that supposed to mean?

ANDREW. You're getting pissy with me because I won't make a decision for you.

SUZANNA. No. I'm asking you to take a firm position. Don't be hurt —

ANDREW. I'm not hurt. I know when you lash out at me, the anger isn't really about me.

SUZANNA. It isn't?

ANDREW. No. It's "why isn't my dad here when I need him?" It's still this really primal rage in you — *(Suzanna makes a dismissive gesture: swats the air or crinkles her face.)*

SUZANNA. Now you're being a writer and, like, trying to make a shit situation seem existential. Which also doesn't help me.

ANDREW. Wow.

SUZANNA. Andrew, if I was in an accident and my head was bleeding, you would have to make a decision for me.

ANDREW. Fine. Right now your head's not bleeding. Your head is fine and capable and … totally cute. Even when obnoxious words come out of it.

SUZANNA. Kiss me? *(They kiss. It's a good kiss. There's real love and passion here.)* What I said about you being a writer? That wasn't meant to be bitchy. Is this our first emergency as husband and wife?

ANDREW. I think so. *(Pause.)* Yeah, I think it is. What do you want to do?

SUZANNA. *(After a beat.)* Call Max. *(Remembering.)* Max. Shit! What time is it? We should cancel with Max and Becky.

ANDREW. Max is probably on his way. I can cancel Becky, but …

SUZANNA. No. If we have Max, we need Becky. He's already resistant to the whole "blind date" thing. We can't abort the mission.

ANDREW. I thought you said he stopped being resistant.

SUZANNA. Let's just introduce them and send them off on their date. I can't be social when I'm this worried.

ANDREW. No. If you're backing out of dinner, we need to cancel with Becky.

SUZANNA. Why?

ANDREW. I just ... The plan was a double-date, with me there to, you know, facilitate a supportive —

SUZANNA. Oh, no. Wait. Why does she need support?

ANDREW. Everyone needs support. And she's ... sorta delicate.

SUZANNA. Oh, fuck you, Andrew. What's wrong with her?

ANDREW. Whoa. You need to stop it, like, now.

SUZANNA. Stop what?

ANDREW. Come on, Susie, we've been over this. I didn't grow up with people sniping and accusing ...

SUZANNA. OK, fine. Tell me the truth about Becky.

ANDREW. She started temping in my office a month ago. I've told you all I know.

SUZANNA. How is she delicate?

ANDREW. She's just at a transition point in her life. She's in a kind of melancholic place ...

SUZANNA. Melancholic. Great. You tell me this now.

ANDREW. Can you stop fixating on my words? Becky is a great catch and she's available because she's in a transitional life space.

SUZANNA. I better warn Max.

ANDREW. Don't. I already warned Becky.

SUZANNA. About what?

ANDREW. I told her ... His coarse delivery belies a rich interior life.

SUZANNA. You've met Max — what — twice?

ANDREW. Exactly. He's a tough first meet. Second time, I liked him. You know, I could drive you to Florida. Miss work Monday, back on Tuesday ...

SUZANNA. Take off Monday? Bullshit, you'll take off Monday.

ANDREW. You want to rephrase that?

SUZANNA. *(After a beat.)* I love you so much. This is the one and only thing that drives me crazy. That you would just blow off work ...

24

ANDREW. Blow off? It's a medical emergency with my mother-in-law.

SUZANNA. You're not working for Jasper and Hermione at the coffee collective anymore. This is a real job.

ANDREW. Oh, this is a "real job" because I wear a suit and it sounds good to your mom and Max. I'm a fucking office manager.

SUZANNA. No. It's a "real job" because you make twice the hourly wage you made at that fucking coffee collective.

ANDREW. When your mom fell down the stairs, Jasper and Hermione — who I know you have no respect for — told me take all the time you need —

SUZANNA. Well, they can do that. They make coffee for a living.

ANDREW. You have class issues.

SUZANNA. No. I have a newly sobering view of how much money it takes to get by in America since my dad died.

ANDREW. (After a beat.) OK. I've been thinking about that and … We don't need two bedrooms. I like having a room to write in, but we could get by in a one-bedroom or a studio …

SUZANNA. Studio? Andrew, we talked to Max. With your new job and me picking up extra work, we're living within our means.

ANDREW. Right, but I can't get any writing done and I hate my job.

SUZANNA. So, you want to move us into a studio, so you can serve coffee … Is that where this is going?

ANDREW. Just until I finish my book and you get your degree. It's not — (Suzanna's phone rings. She picks it up, looks at the number …)

SUZANNA. Oh, this better be my mother … It's Max. (Answering.) Hey, I can't talk, I'm waiting for my mom to call. (Pause.) It's in Andrew's name. Porter. (Hangs up.)

ANDREW. OK, before he gets here … I don't want to leave this unfinished … (The buzzer buzzes. As Suzanna goes to it …)

SUZANNA. Let's talk about it with Max.

ANDREW. No! Susie, this is private. (Suzanna rushes to Andrew and kisses him hard on the mouth.) Is that your way of saying you'll live in a studio?

SUZANNA. No. That means I love you, and fighting is OK. It doesn't change that. (Suzanna rushes to the door, opens it, and steps out to look for Max. Calling out:) Are you ninety? It's two flights of stairs …

MAX. (Entering.) I had to muscle past five generations of Portuguese people frying fish.

25

SUZANNA. They're our landlords. Don't be racist.

MAX. It's nice to see you, too. What the hell is wrong?

SUZANNA. The usual shit. You want a glass of wine?

MAX. Sure. I brought a bottle. *(Max gives Suzanna a bag with a bottle of wine in it. As she takes it to Andrew who will open it ...)*

SUZANNA. Our wine is not shit, Max.

MAX. Don't be hostile. I brought a nice wine because it's your ... six-week anniversary? Hello, Andrew. Congratulations.

ANDREW. Hey, Max.

SUZANNA. It's three months, asshole. That's not a real anniversary. Next week is, though. We can drink on that. *(After a beat.)* Max?

MAX. What?

SUZANNA. Next week?

MAX. I don't know. What is next week?

SUZANNA. Come on!

MAX. What is it ... Flag Day? I don't know.

ANDREW. *(After a beat.)* Her dad's death ... It's a year ...

MAX. OK. Right. You don't celebrate that, though. That's what threw me.

SUZANNA. You acknowledge it. You're coming over, right?

MAX. I ... What day is it?

SUZANNA. Forget it. Andrew and I are gonna commemorate it. If you can't even remember the date, I don't want you here.

MAX. Commemorate? It's not the fucking bicentennial.

ANDREW. "Commemorate" is probably the wrong word. It was my idea. When I was in high school, a kid in my class died. And when the anniversary came around, people had a lot of feelings about it, so —

MAX. I'm sure they did. They were in fucking high school.

SUZANNA. Max.

ANDREW. We threw a party. It sounds weird, but it really helped shift us from mourning to, you know, celebrating his life.

MAX. OK. I'll come. Should I make a mix tape, or ...

SUZANNA. If you're gonna make fun of it, don't come.

MAX. Are you having your period? What the fuck is wrong with you?

SUZANNA. What's usually wrong? My mother ...

MAX. Oh. Well, in that case, we should start drinking and change the subject.

SUZANNA. You know, Max ... This is why you don't have a girl-friend.

MAX. Your mother is why I don't have a girlfriend? Actually, there's probably some truth to that.

SUZANNA. No. You don't have a girlfriend, because you ask me what's wrong, then when I tell you, you're all "nothin' I can do."

MAX. *(To Andrew.)* Is it all you hoped and dreamed of ... being married to her?

ANDREW. It's great. How do you like Boston? You getting settled?

MAX. Boston is ... For four months, it's fine.

ANDREW. What is it you're doing ... again ...

MAX. I'm opening a Boston office for my company.

ANDREW. Yeah? Which part of the city are you —

MAX. *(Overlapping and dismissing.)* That's a whole ... I'm still sorting the details out. *(And changing the subject ...)* Look. Susie. You and your mother ... It's like the Middle East. Bad situation, not gonna change. So why talk about it?

SUZANNA. Because ... It begins with an "e," ends with a "y." You can't do it ...

MAX. Nurture? No. Empathy! Right! Women and empathy, man ... This is just like the date I had last week ... The dance professor who wanted to talk about the Iraq war ...

ANDREW. You can't talk about the Iraq war?

MAX. For a few minutes, fine. But there's nothing I can do about it, and there is definitely nothing Annabell the dance professor can do about it, so —

ANDREW. Wait, you can't really believe there's nothing anyone can do.

MAX. Let me clarify. I send a lot of money to people whose job it is to do the right thing —

SUZANNA. The Democrats?

MAX. No, NAMBLA. Of course, the Democrats, stupid.

ANDREW. So people who don't have money can't exert any impact?

MAX. That's not what I'm saying. I'm saying I do my share ... I give away ten percent of my income to people whose job it is to solve this problem. It's their job. It's not mine. And I don't want my dinner ruined.

ANDREW. So what did you say to her?

MAX. Oh ... She wanted to tell me about this protest at Harvard. Some artists emoting against the war bullshit ...

SUZANNA. You told her it was stupid and pointless.

MAX. I did not say it was stupid. I did say it was pointless.

SUZANNA. You're a jerk.

ANDREW. *(To Max.)* You're probably right, but you don't want to say that on a first date.

MAX. Wait. Did you just agree with me?

ANDREW. It depends on how you said it. I used to go to those protests at Brown, but ... I started to feel like they weren't really about the war. No one important was watching, we were just ... assuaging our guilt and getting laid. I feel like ... Do something real or do nothing, you know?

SUZANNA. Now, if you say it like that, it's OK ...

MAX. Which do you do?

ANDREW. What?

MAX. About the war. Do you do something real or do you do nothing?

ANDREW. Umm ... I don't do as much as I should. There's a group at Brown that sends books to the troops —

MAX. Oh, those poor troops. The Brown kids are sending them books ...

SUZANNA. The troops are not illiterate, Max.

MAX. No, they're not. But when you live in fear of dirty bombs and torture, you do not want a used, highlighted copy of *To the Fucking Lighthouse*!

ANDREW. Max, I need you to take, like, a mellower tone with Becky.

SUZANNA. She's delicate.

ANDREW. She is not delicate! Just ... Max, it's not, like, emasculating to open yourself to another person's experience ...

MAX. I don't know, Andrew. That sounded pretty fucking womanly.

SUZANNA. Tell him what to say. Give him actual words.

ANDREW. You could say something like, "Wow, that's kind of outside my experience, so I would need for you to say more."

MAX. *(To Suzanna; genuine.)* Is that ... Don't tell me he snared you talking like that?

SUZANNA. I love it. It makes me weak. *(Andrew's phone rings and he answers it.)*

ANDREW. Hello? *(Pause.)* Hey! *(Pause.)* Sorry. It's Porter. Just buzz — *(Pause.)* Oh, sure. Stay there. I'll meet you. Bye. *(He hangs up.)* That's Becky. I'm gonna go get her.

SUZANNA. Why don't you just have her buzz?

ANDREW. She was actually calling from the mini-mart. She didn't know my last name either.

SUZANNA. Why is she at the mini-mart?

ANDREW. She doesn't have a cell phone. I'm gonna go get her. *(Andrew grabs his coat and leaves.)*

MAX. Is my date ... Amish?

SUZANNA. No. You're here! I'm so happy! *(Suzanna grabs Max and bear-hugs him. He enjoys it, if stiffly.)*

MAX. I am here. You ... really do live in Rhode Island.

SUZANNA. What's that supposed to mean?

MAX. *(Sniffing his lapel.)* I've got Portuguese fish-fry all over me.

SUZANNA. My landlords are so sweet. When we moved in, they made us wedding soup.

MAX. And you ate it?

SUZANNA. Of course. It's not like New York, Max. Landlords don't kill you to end your rent control.

MAX. I'm not rent-controlled. I own my place. I may buy a building, did I tell you?

SUZANNA. Your building?

MAX. No. In Brooklyn. So when you're ready to leave this little Portuguese fishing village, I'll cut you a good deal.

SUZANNA. I don't know if Andrew wants to live in New York. Listen ... I should have asked you this before, and please don't tell Andrew I didn't. You and that woman are totally done, right?

MAX. That woman?

SUZANNA. Christa. It's over, right? You're available?

MAX. I told you it's over.

SUZANNA. I know. It's just ... She was around longer than the others, so I wanted to double-check ...

MAX. "The others"?

SUZANNA. Come on, Max. You're a short-timer. You get the three-month itch. That was a really long relationship for you.

MAX. It was three months. I love that you're incapable of even simple math.

SUZANNA. It felt longer.

MAX. Well. I don't move as fast as you and Junior ...

SUZANNA. If you call him Junior to his face, I'll kill you —

MAX. A four-month courtship and a Vegas wedding. That's fast. And he is your junior.

SUZANNA. By four years! Thirty-one/thirty-five ... It's nothing.

MAX. He's thirty-one? I guess he seems younger because he's so … indie-rock.

SUZANNA. Stop it.

MAX. It's not bad, it's just a cultural difference. Hey — when he comes back … five hundred dollars says he thinks 401(k) is a band.

SUZANNA. No, don't. That's mean. But speaking of money … Don't tell Andrew I asked you this …

MAX. I'm keeping a lot of secrets here …

SUZANNA. Andrew is, like, not that happy at his job. He wants to take a pay cut and move us to a smaller place.

MAX. What's the question?

SUZANNA. Could we stay in this apartment if our income was … less?

MAX. How much less? Don't answer. Look, you can do whatever you want. You can take a ten-thousand-dollar honeymoon. You can buy a nice car. But when your money's gone, it's gone.

SUZANNA. So the answer is no?

MAX. It's a judgment call. If you'd married a medical student, I'd say go ahead, live a little. But Andrew … I don't see any guarantee of earning power.

SUZANNA. That's not the measure of a man's worth, Max.

MAX. You didn't ask me about his worth! You asked me about money.

SUZANNA. Sorry. I know it's a judgment call. But your judgment's better than mine, you know?

MAX. Oh, I know. *(After a beat.)* Look at a couple cheaper places. Come back to me with actual numbers and I'll tell you what to do.

SUZANNA. *(Hugging him.)* Thank you. *(The door opens. Andrew enters followed by Becky, thirty-four.)*

ANDREW. Hey! Everyone … This is Becky. Becky, this is my wife, Suzanna. This is Max. Let me take your coat … *(Max moves to shake Becky's hand as she takes off her coat to reveal a dress. The dress is not wildly over the top and should not function as a sight gag. The faux pas of the dress is a maddeningly subtle one … It's lovely, just a bit too much for this night and these people. Maybe it's a cocktail dress tiered like a layer cake. Maybe it's that and pink [or yellow or lavender]. It's a great dress for another occasion and Becky looks great in it. For this night and these people, however, she's overdressed, and she realizes this almost immediately. The confidence she cultivated alone in her apartment evaporates.)*

BECKY. Nice to meet you all. Or ... both.

MAX. Wow. You look like ... a birthday cake.

SUZANNA. No, she doesn't. Ignore him. It's nice to meet you, Becky.

MAX. I was complimenting her! It wouldn't kill you to wear a dress once a year ...

BECKY. I'm totally overdressed.

ANDREW. No, you're not. Do you drink red wine?

BECKY. Yes. *(Awkward moment between Max and Becky. First looks, first mental assessments.)*

MAX. You're very ... Your face is pink. Have you been drinking this evening?

BECKY. No! I just ... I called the cab too early, so I had to walk around and kill some time. It's really cold ...

ANDREW. You should have just come over. We weren't doing anything.

SUZANNA. Yeah, we were just fighting. I'm actually not dressed yet. I'm gonna change.

MAX. Why were you fighting?

SUZANNA. I told you. My mom. *(Remembering.)* Shit! My mom! *(To Max.)* You totally distracted me. I'm gonna try and call her ... *(Suzanna leaves to change and call her mother. Awkward silence. This would be the moment for the newly-introduced couple to begin a gentle Q and A ...)*

MAX. Warming up any?

BECKY. Yes! I guess that was silly of me. It's just ... You know how Providence cabs are. Or ... You don't; you live in New York.

ANDREW. I should have picked you up. I feel like an idiot ...

MAX. Is something wrong with your car?

BECKY. Yeah. I mean, I don't have one.

MAX. Is that ... an economic necessity or a life choice?

BECKY. Life choice?

MAX. Are you, like, a militant environmentalist? Do you oppose cars in theory or ...

BECKY. Oh, no. I just don't have any money. *(An awkward moment.)* I mean I have some. I have money. *(A beat. Max does a little mental math on this exchange and ... turns to Andrew.)*

MAX. So what's up with Susan? Why is Susie calling her?

ANDREW. Her mother's health insurance company called. *(To Becky.)* My wife and her mother have the same name: Suzanna Slater.

BECKY. Oh. That must get confusing.

ANDREW. It's actually pretty manageable with nicknames. Her mother goes by Susan, Suzanna kinda defaults to Susie. If we have a female child, I don't know what's left for her.

BECKY. There's ... Suky.

MAX. Too Asian.

BECKY. Actually, Edie Sedgwick ... The Warhol model? Her sister was Suky. Suky Sedgwick.

MAX. Really?

BECKY. Yes.

MAX. Do you know the lineage of all the Warhol models, or just —

ANDREW. So, the insurance people called here. They realized they had the wrong Suzanna Slater and they hung up. And Susan's in Florida with her boyfriend, Lester. *(Suzanna returns in a dress ... more monochromatic and sophisticated than Becky's — best she could do, having legitimately tried to match Becky.)*

SUZANNA. She's still not picking up. And she's in Florida with Fucko-the-Rentboy so God only knows what's become of her.

MAX. You called Lester?

SUZANNA. Hell no, I did not call Lester! It's still early ... I think I should fly down there and find out what happened.

MAX. Did you call the hotel?

SUZANNA. I don't know where they're staying.

MAX. So what the fuck are you gonna to do when you get there?

SUZANNA. Just ... find her. Key West can't be that big.

MAX. Uhhh ... It's big enough. Why haven't you called Lester?

SUZANNA. What kind of stupid fucking question is that? You know why.

MAX. Andrew, why won't she call Lester?

SUZANNA. Max, fuck off. I made my boundary very clear.

ANDREW. You guys ... Becky doesn't know any of these people, so maybe we should stop ...

BECKY. Oh, no ... It's OK. Family problems are just ... God, I don't even speak to my family.

MAX. Really? Why is that?

BECKY. Umm ... It's a pretty long story.

MAX. You don't speak to them, or they don't speak to you?

BECKY. It's basically mutual.

SUZANNA. Oh, don't look at her like that's so weird. I wish I could do it. So do you.

MAX. Yeah, but we'd never actually do it; they're our parents.

Andrew, call Lester.'

ANDREW. Susie says we have the same boundaries because we're married.

MAX. *(Gets out his phone.)* Wow. It's a good thing I showed up. I have no boundaries at all, Becky. Did they tell you that?

BECKY. No ...

MAX. *(To Andrew.)* Did you try to talk some sense into her?

ANDREW. I offered to drive her down ...

MAX. And do what when you get there? What the hell is wrong with you two?

ANDREW. I didn't know she didn't know —

SUZANNA. Max, Key West is not that big!

MAX. Correct. It's a small town with about nine hundred bed-and-breakfasts.

ANDREW. There's probably only one hospital.

MAX. Did you call this one hospital? *(No answer.)* Of course, you didn't. You're both idiots.

SUZANNA. Max —

MAX. *(Dialing his phone.)* Sit down, drink your wine. It's ringing. Lester! Lester, my man, Max Garrett here. How the hell are you? *(Pause.)* I'm very well. How are you and Susan? *(Pause.)* Well, that's great to hear. So the reason I'm calling is that you are a lying sack of shit. What happened to Susan? *(Pause.)* Uh-huh. *(Pause; rolls eyes.)* So she's OK? *(Pause.)* Good. I — *(Pause.)* Suzanna? Fuck Suzanna. This is a conversation between men and I am not a snitch. *(Mouth away from receiver, Max shakes his head, mouths "stupid, stupid, stupid" as he walks into Andrew and Suzanna's bedroom and closes the door. Suzanna moves to follow him, Andrew cuts her off.)*

ANDREW. Susie. Don't. Just let him get the whole story.

SUZANNA. I'm sorry, Becky. This is completely rude ... I just don't know if it's serious or not ...

BECKY. It's no problem! Is Max, like, related to you?

SUZANNA. Not exactly. My parents kind of adopted him.

BECKY. Oh! His parents are dead?

SUZANNA. Only his mom. His dad's just ... useless.

BECKY. I don't really feel I'm making a good impression.

ANDREW. You're doing great.

SUZANNA. Please. I'm the one making a bad impression. If you're not at your best it's only because I'm not at mine.

BECKY. So you agree I'm not at my best ...

SUZANNA. No! I'm just apologizing. For letting my problems dominate the room. See, my parents would never let that happen.

ANDREW. Southern gentility ...

SUZANNA. It's not that ...

BECKY. Yeah, my mom's from the South and she's not gentle at all ...

SUZANNA. Remember in Greek mythology ... The gods judge you by how well you treat the strangers who come to your door ... What is that called?

ANDREW. The guest/host code?

SUZANNA. It's got a Greek name, too ... *(A silence Becky wishes she could fill, but ... She refuses to be rattled. She's promised herself she'll project bright, light, and confident.)*

BECKY. I didn't read those myths, I don't think. Do a lot of ... strangers come to the door?

SUZANNA. Yeah. They're always burning and pillaging each other. So everyone is homeless and hungry at some point. Do you want some more wine, Becky?

BECKY. A little ... Thanks. *(As Andrew pours her wine.)* Is there anything I should do or not do, as far as Max ...

ANDREW. Just be yourself.

SUZANNA. Inasmuch as you can, don't show him any weakness.

ANDREW. No. Susie ... That's not helpful ...

BECKY. Do I seem weak ... so far?

SUZANNA. No, no, no. All I'm saying is ... First date. Everybody's nervous. We all have a *thing* we fall back on when we're nervous ... Flirting or bragging or whatever. His thing is bullying. Just try not to give him an opening.

MAX. *(Reentering.)* OK. I really don't like to admit that I'm wrong. But my God, he is a loser.

SUZANNA. See?

MAX. They were in the pool at the hotel and your mom "forgot" her cane up in the room.

SUZANNA. Because Lester makes her self-destructive.

MAX. Oh, shut the fuck up. If that's what your psychology program is teaching you ...

SUZANNA. She forgot her cane and she fell. Is it bad?

MAX. No. She tripped. Her knees are bruised. The hotel overreacted. She is not "self-destructive," Suzanna —

ANDREW. *(To Becky.)* Susie's mom has MS. Multiple —

34

MAX. Andrew, give the girl some credit. She knows what MS is.

BECKY. I don't know a lot. I know Jerry Lewis does that telethon ...

SUZANNA. That's muscular dystrophy.

BECKY. Oh, my God, I know that! I don't know why I said that ...

SUZANNA. Refusing to use her cane is self-destructive.

ANDREW. MS is multiple sclerosis ...

BECKY. I know that. I just ... Nerves.

MAX. You're nervous?

BECKY. A little ...

SUZANNA. If my mom's fine, what did you have to go in the other room for?

MAX. Because ... Sometimes in a crisis, you learn things about people that you didn't know.

SUZANNA. What did we learn?

MAX. Lester's credit cards are all maxed out. He can't use them.

SUZANNA. He's a huge loser. That's not a surprise.

MAX. Well, it surprised your mother. She gave him money to pay off his credit cards and he spent it on something else.

SUZANNA. What — drugs?

MAX. No. Some kind of editing equipment. For his film.

SUZANNA. You fucked up, Max.

MAX. No, I didn't. Your mother called me, she wanted five thousand dollars sent to Lester's credit card company. I said great, fine. Then I sent the money to Lester. You see what I did there?

SUZANNA. Yes. You fucked up.

MAX. No, stupid! I protected you. You should be down on your knees thanking me —

SUZANNA. (Overlapping.) How is putting thousands of dollars in Lester's hands protecting me?

MAX. Anyone? Anyone?

BECKY. (After a beat.) You set him up to fail. (Surprised eyes on Becky.) Instead of paying his creditors, you paid him. You tested him, knowing he would fail.

MAX. Very good, Becky! So now he has to beg your mother's forgiveness. That little movie he wants to make ... I just put that baby in turnaround.

SUZANNA. You're a genius. I'm so sorry.

MAX. Oh, rest assured I will do whatever it takes to protect you.

SUZANNA. I know. I shouldn't doubt you.

ANDREW. So, if Susan's OK ... Maybe we can kinda start the

night over …

SUZANNA. Yes! Let's do that. Let's start over.

MAX. Starting over. Great. So. Becky. What are you doing in Providence? Did you go to Brown?

BECKY. I actually did go to Brown … briefly. But I dropped out.

MAX. So that makes you … smart, but lazy.

ANDREW. Max.

BECKY. No, it's OK. I got into Brown because I lived in Rhode Island —

ANDREW. That's so not true. You're super-smart; you were not a regional quota-filler.

MAX. So you're actually from here? Congratulations. On losing the accent.

BECKY. We moved here when I was eleven. I was born in North Carolina, actually.

MAX. Well, my congratulations holds. That's a pretty fucking awful accent, too.

BECKY. Right. Thanks.

MAX. *(To Suzanna, brightening.)* Wait wait wait … Tell that story.

SUZANNA. What story?

MAX. The bubbla …

SUZANNA. Andrew's heard it.

ANDREW. Yeah … I have …

MAX. Becky hasn't. You gotta hear this … *(It's a story Max and Suzanna find hilarious. It's a fun accent to imitate and they both love a good "Suzanna's so dumb … " story.)*

SUZANNA. OK, so I work with a lot of kids at the clinic. I'm a grad student in psychology. And we do these intake interviews …

MAX. I hate how women tell stories. Susie's interviewing a kid and the kid says …

SUZANNA. Wheasdabubbla. And I'm like … I'm reading all these amazing cases where the therapist was like Sherlock Holmes cracking the code and saving the day —

MAX. Mother of fucking God, get to the point. Wheasdabubbla.

SUZANNA. So. I wrote it down to analyze later, and then she yells, "WHEASDAFUCKINBUBBLA?!" And I hear a thud … the secretary's chair hitting the wall. I poke my head out the door and the secretary says …

MAX. Givvasomewota.

SUZANNA. Water. Bubbla is bubbler, which is Rhode Islandese

for water fountain.

BECKY. So did you give her some water?

SUZANNA. Yes. I gave her some water and she threw it at me. And then I started to get it.

MAX. Please don't tell me you drew some fancy conclusion from a kid throwing water.

SUZANNA. It wasn't "fancy," but ...

BECKY. But it gave you this amazing clue. You could see that —

MAX. Amazing clue?

ANDREW. Jesus, Max. Let Becky talk.

BECKY. It just seems like she got angry because she wasn't being heard. She didn't ask for water; she asked you where the bubbler was. You weren't listening to her.

SUZANNA. Well —

MAX. That is such horseshit.

ANDREW. It's not horseshit. The kids at that clinic have some pretty serious problems.

SUZANNA. I never said they didn't, Andrew.

ANDREW. Not that the story isn't amusing out of context. I get that.

SUZANNA. We should drop it anyway. Max has a personal bias against psychotherapy.

MAX. It can't be personal. I've never been in therapy.

SUZANNA. I know. Say that a little louder in case Becky missed it.

MAX. Becky, I HAVE NEVER BEEN IN THERAPY.

BECKY. I have.

MAX. And did it cure you of whatever ... problem brought you there?

BECKY. Umm ... I went a few times for a few different issues.

MAX. OK. So ... To recap, you dropped out of college, you're not on speaking terms with your family, and you have no money. Sounds to me like the therapy didn't work.

ANDREW. Max —

BECKY. *(Flirting?)* How do you know? You didn't see me before I went.

SUZANNA. Oooh ... She told you.

MAX. She definitely did ... tell me. Anything else you want to reveal here ... STDs, felony convictions ...

BECKY. I just have ... mistakes. Family stuff. Don't we all have that? Don't you?

MAX. No, I've led a wholly unblemished and exemplary life. I

37

will, however, own up to being hungry.

BECKY. *(Is Max making an effort to connect?)* Hungry? Yeah … I feel that, too. Do you know what you're hungry for?

MAX. Tonight, I'm thinking lasagna. Can we get out of here?

SUZANNA. Don't kill me …

MAX. Oh, no.

SUZANNA. I want to talk to my mom.

MAX. Susan is fine!

SUZANNA. I want to call and provoke her. If she fights with me, then I'll know she's OK. Give me a pass tonight. Andrew can go.

ANDREW. You know what? The vibe I'm feeling is maybe you two go have dinner; Susie and I will veg out here. Is that too weird and awkward?

BECKY. No, no. It's fine. If it's OK with Max, I mean.

MAX. We don't need you two to have fun. Fuck you two. We're out of here. *(Everyone rises. As coats are retrieved and put on …)*

SUZANNA. Have fun. Be safe.

ANDREW. You know where you're going?

MAX. I have no idea. But my date lives here, right? She knows restaurants.

BECKY. I do. I mean, I don't really eat out ever, but …

MAX. Of course you don't. *(Off her mild recoil … he touches her.)* Kidding. Kidding. *(To Suzanna.)* Did you put any thought at all into this evening or is there a Zagat's New England you can throw at me on my way out?

SUZANNA. I know. I'm sorry. Andrew, give him that Federal Hill map …

MAX. I don't need a map; I need a recommendation.

ANDREW. No, this is a map *with* recommendations. It comes in your Brown orientation materials. That's a really good idea. Why don't I show you … *(Andrew gestures for Max to follow him into the office, and he does, awkwardly. A moment's silence between the women.)*

BECKY. So, what … happened to her — the girl?

SUZANNA. The girl?

BECKY. The bubbla girl.

SUZANNA. Oh! Right. I don't know. I only saw her that one time.

BECKY. Why?

SUZANNA. I think she was an eval. We do a lot of evaluations for the public school system.

BECKY. That must be very hard.

SUZANNA. Which part? It's all hard.

BECKY. Seeing each other only once. For me that would be very hard. *(A slight, odd tension. Then Max and Andrew return ...)*

ANDREW. Just have fun, you know ...

MAX. Fun? Andrew here has given me a list of restaurants so exceptional that one must ... *(Reading.)* Book in advance for commencement and campus dance.

SUZANNA. That just means they're expensive.

ANDREW. I circled the ones that aren't, like, weird and fussy.

MAX. *(To Becky.)* Andrew's incredibly nervous. Tell him you're OK and you're going to have fun. *(Becky smiles at this and turns to Andrew.)*

BECKY. I'm OK. And I'm going to have fun. *(A beat before Max and Becky leave. The idea is to suggest [without forecasting "doom"] a frozen moment after which these lives will change. Maybe lights go down last on Becky, standing at a bit of a distance from the others ... She believes this night can still go well. And we should, too.)*

End of Act One

ACT TWO

Scene 1

Downtown Providence (outdoors). Two days later, Monday. Becky and Andrew have left the office to get coffee or hot dogs.

We begin with Becky alone onstage.

BECKY. *(Rehearsing.)* Something bad happened on my date with Max. *(Andrew enters and hands Becky her drink/food.)*
ANDREW. Here you go. So ... Susie is trying to play it cool, not call Max for forty-eight hours after your date. But she's, like, twitching to make the call.
BECKY. Andrew, something happened on my date with Max.
ANDREW. Yeah?
BECKY. We were robbed. We were robbed with a gun!
ANDREW. Robbed? Where?
BECKY. We went to The Decatur for a nightcap. Andrew, I feel so stupid!
ANDREW. Why?
BECKY. I'd never been there! You said it was cool, so I said it was cool. Jesus! I hate myself!
ANDREW. Wait. A stranger robbed you, right? Why would you hate yourself?
BECKY. We parked too far away, and it's a bad area ...
ANDREW. It's not bad ...
BECKY. It's bad, Andrew! A man came up to us with a gun and we gave him our wallets, but neither of us had much cash, so Max said we should walk back to the car ...
ANDREW. Wait. Did the guy ask for more or did Max volunteer, "I'm rich, I have money in my car"?
BECKY. He ... volunteered.
ANDREW. That's really stupid.

40

BECKY. There was a gun pointing at us! He was trying to keep us alive.

ANDREW. I'm sorry.

BECKY. The guy held the gun on me while Max went into the car ... Andrew, I thought I was going to die! Max gave him two hundred dollars and a camera. Then he left.

ANDREW. He left. He didn't hurt you. Rape you ...

BECKY. No. Oh my God! Don't even say that!

ANDREW. So you're OK?

BECKY. No, I'm not OK.

ANDREW. I just mean ... Thank God you weren't hurt ...

BECKY. Don't tell me I'm not hurt!

ANDREW. Of course! Becky, what can I do?

BECKY. Can you give me a hug? Would that be OK?

ANDREW. Oh my God, yes. Here ... *(It's awkward with the drink/food. Delay getting into the hug lends a tension, a charge. He pats her back, soothes her.)* You're trembling ...

BECKY. *(Breaking the hug.)* I feel like a leaf! I'm alone ... There's not enough of me ... I just get blown around and torn up and I'm *trying*, but I can't make it stop! Do you know what I mean?

ANDREW. I ... can't even imagine. *(He initiates a second hug, holds her a moment, then breaks it ...)* You should talk to someone. You have a therapist, right?

BECKY. I haven't seen her in years. My parents helped me pay for that and now ... They're not speaking to me and I'm uninsured and completely broke.

ANDREW. Just ... Tell her you need a few sessions, but you can't pay right away ...

BECKY. A few sessions. That's like eight hundred dollars. I can't afford a meatball sub at lunch. I'm eating peanut butter sandwiches every day. I'm sorry. I have made a mess of my life. It's not your problem. *(Pause.)* No one in my family speaks to me, you know.

ANDREW. I know. I don't know why, but I'm sure they're the problem, not you.

BECKY. You don't know the whole story. We should go back to work.

ANDREW. Let me call Susie and get the name of a clinic with a sliding scale.

BECKY. No ...

ANDREW. It's no problem.

BECKY. No, Andrew! I don't want ghetto therapy!

ANDREW. *(After a beat.)* OK. What ... What can I do?

BECKY. Max and I haven't spoken since that night. He's the only person who knows what I'm feeling and he won't return my calls.

ANDREW. Maybe he lost his cell phone. He hasn't called Susie either.

BECKY. It didn't happen to Susie! It happened to me. He should call me.

ANDREW. He should, you're right. Susie can make that happen.

BECKY. Tonight? I want it to happen tonight.

ANDREW. OK, tonight. She'll make it happen tonight.

Scene 2

That same evening (Monday). Max and Suzanna in Max's Boston hotel room. It's a nicer hotel than the hotel in the first scene. Boutique-y. One more star.

SUZANNA. I just figured I should drive up here, smooth things over face-to-face before they get any worse.

MAX. Your husband's a dick.

SUZANNA. He just asked you to call Becky. Why are you being so weird?

MAX. I'm weird because I won't call her?

SUZANNA. Well ... yes. This is *all* really weird, Max. I find out secondhand from Andrew that you were held up at gunpoint. Why didn't you call me?

MAX. Are you the police? Are you in a position to get my camera back?

SUZANNA. You need support. Look, I know from my work that men can experience shame when they're victimized ...

MAX. Oh, no ...

SUZANNA. Don't cut me off. Both times your father got arrested, I begged you —

MAX. My father's not in trouble anymore.

SUZANNA. Well, that's ... good. But ... God, Max. Why don't you call me when you're hurting?

MAX. This isn't hurt, it's frustration.

SUZANNA. Fine! Talk to me about it. We're friends.

MAX. My frustration is with you.

SUZANNA. With me?

MAX. Yes. My father is a white-collar criminal. He is an unrepentant repeat offender. Between my father's stealing and your father's squandering, it's amazing that I have any time or any money for myself. When you force me to talk about things that make me unhappy, you pollute my leisure time. You become part of the fucking problem.

SUZANNA. *(Not what she expected.)* OK, I respect that.

MAX. I'll buy you a steak and a soufflé if you drop the subject.

SUZANNA. Great. But first will you please call Becky?

MAX. No!

SUZANNA. It's one phone call. Why —

MAX. Why? Because that's my choice. It's like you marrying Andrew. Friends don't have to agree with each other's choices, but they do have to respect them.

SUZANNA. *(After a beat.)* OK, let's just do this. You're angry at me for marrying Andrew and I don't understand why.

MAX. I'm not angry. I just think you should have consulted me before you flew to Vegas and married your ski buddy.

SUZANNA. Wow. You really are angry. Is it because ... Is it because we slept together that one time?

MAX. *(After a beat.)* Well ...

SUZANNA. I knew it! You can't say sex won't change anything. It always does.

MAX. Not always. When you've known the person twenty-five years, it ... Yes.

SUZANNA. You told me it wouldn't change anything!

MAX. Sex makes men territorial. Forget it. It's not rational.

SUZANNA. Let's call it what it is, OK? We opened the door. After two decades, we opened the door and neither of us walked through it.

MAX. Well. I turned around, you had a husband in the fucking doorway ...

SUZANNA. That was months later! You started dating Christa before I —

MAX. A month after we ... Were you waiting for me to walk through the door? This isn't Jane Austen's England, Susie. You could've walked through it, too.

43

SUZANNA. Right. We both could have done it and neither of us did. So I think … There's our answer.

MAX. OK.

SUZANNA. There's our answer. We love each other, but not in the way Andrew and I —

MAX. Fuck Andrew. He is way out of line calling me at work —

SUZANNA. You're angry because Andrew —

MAX. I'm angry that you two morons put me in this position!

SUZANNA. Max, we didn't rob you.

MAX. Oh, fuck the robbery. It's a nonevent and I'm over it.

SUZANNA. Well, Becky isn't over it.

MAX. Clearly. She's been calling me all weekend.

SUZANNA. She had a gun pointed at her. It's traumatic.

MAX. For her, maybe. Not for me.

SUZANNA. Max, that's insane.

MAX. No. My reaction is not insane. In life … I'm gonna do this visually because I know you can't do math. *(Indicating.)* This wall is your perfect life. You and everyone you know living happy lives until you die of old age in each others' arms.

SUZANNA. No one has that life.

MAX. Shut up, I'm still talking. That wall over there is as bad as it gets. What is that wall for you?

SUZANNA. You know what it is, Max. The underground sex-torture dungeon.

MAX. Consider these two walls … and the points in between — chair, table, lamp, phone — being all variety of life shit in between torture in a dungeon and happy all the time. Where on this trajectory would you place a three-minute hold-up in which no one got hurt?

SUZANNA. Max, that's not fair.

MAX. It is fair. You and I have been through hell with our parents. Cancer, MS, jail, death … What happened to Becky and me … It doesn't even rank.

SUZANNA. Say, for the sake of argument, you're right. What does it cost you to talk to her?

MAX. I don't want to. And I don't have to.

SUZANNA. OK, forget responsibility. How about kindness?

MAX. Why me? Where are her fucking friends?

SUZANNA. She wants to talk to you because you were there.

MAX. Well, that I don't believe.

SUZANNA. What do you think the reason is?

MAX. She wants a relationship with me.

SUZANNA. Really? After one date?

MAX. Look at her life, look at the dress she wore that night. You fixed me up with a desperate woman.

SUZANNA. She's desperate because she wore a dress?

MAX. She's a thirty-five-year-old office temp with no money, no friends, no relationship, no family ... How the fuck could you set me up with that?

SUZANNA. Wait. You think I set you up with someone who isn't good enough for you?

MAX. I don't think that. That is a fact.

SUZANNA. Max, she's good looking ...

MAX. She's a sad person, Suzanna.

SUZANNA. So? I've been sad. Did it make me undesirable or —

MAX. Romantic relationships are the pairing of equals! That woman is not my equal!

SUZANNA. Please call her, Max.

MAX. What the fuck do you care? You met this girl once.

SUZANNA. I'll give you the script. Tell her that this experience — the hold-up — has shown you that you're not emotionally available enough to be in a relationship. Let her talk about her experience. Wish her well ... It's over.

MAX. None of that is true.

SUZANNA. No, but it's merciful. Sometimes lying is the most humane thing you can do.

MAX. *(After a beat.)* I'll think about it.

Scene 3

Andrew and Becky in Becky's apartment the following night — Tuesday. Andrew has brought beer and a pizza.

BECKY. I'm so sorry. I heard this weird noise and since the hold-up, I'm just ... *(Indicates jittery.)*

ANDREW. It's totally OK.

BECKY. But to make you come running over here … Suzanna must hate me.

ANDREW. No. It's good I got out of the house. She's … studying.

BECKY. Please thank her for speaking with Max on my behalf.

ANDREW. Not that it helped.

BECKY. What did he say — exactly?

ANDREW. A lot of bullshit that has nothing to do with you.

BECKY. Really? If he thinks I'm a loser, I can take it. It's the silence that's so awful …

ANDREW. It's not that.

BECKY. So what is it?

ANDREW. I think he just can't deal with what happened. He's emotionally a very … stunted man.

BECKY. Then why did you set me up with him? *(Awkward beat.)*

ANDREW. I'd met him twice before that night. I trusted Susie …

BECKY. Max wasn't at your wedding?

ANDREW. No … We got married kind of fast. In Las Vegas.

BECKY. Why so fast?

ANDREW. It was just a really intense time.

BECKY. How was it intense?

ANDREW. Susie's life was just … It was seriously, the most epic, Faulknerian chaos I've ever encountered outside a fictional paradigm. *(Pause.)* Did I just sound like a total tool?

BECKY. No, I understand.

ANDREW. Susie's dad had just died. We met on a ski trip and she was so sad. She wore this red parka, you know, and she looked so small against these huge, white mountains. I would look at her and think … I shouldn't tell you, it's weird.

BECKY. Tell me.

ANDREW. I would look at her and think … She's like blood on the snow. Her sadness is wrong, and I want to fix it.

BECKY. I don't think that's weird. You were falling in love.

ANDREW. Sure felt like it. It makes more sense if you knew her then. She was really different. More … delicate.

BECKY. Suzanna? That's hard to imagine.

ANDREW. Oh, I know. She's so much healthier now.

BECKY. She's lucky she found you.

ANDREW. *(After a beat.)* Look, I want to apologize. Susie is blind to Max's flaws, but I —

BECKY. He takes such good care of her.

ANDREW. Well ... They're family. And on paper, Max looks great. He's rich, charismatic, looking to settle down —

BECKY. He's looking to settle down? He said that?

ANDREW. He told Susie, you know, "I'm thirty-six; I'm ready to ... " *(Thinking better.)* "To, I guess be open ... "

BECKY. Wow. I kind of wish you hadn't told me that.

ANDREW. Saying it is one thing. He's never gonna do it.

BECKY. Wait. You fixed me up with someone you think is never going to settle down?

ANDREW. No, no, no —

BECKY. He said he wants to settle down and he meant it, right? You're just trying to save my feelings now by lying —

ANDREW. I'm not lying. I just found out. *(Pause.)* Look. Susie wasn't studying when you called. We were fighting because Susie said that Max is ... a short-timer.

BECKY. What is a "short-timer"?

ANDREW. It's a Vietnam War term. It means guys who go into combat for short stints and don't stay. Max, apparently, only dates women for, like, three months.

BECKY. Oh.

ANDREW. I didn't know that until tonight. Susie said it and I just flipped —

BECKY. She should have told you.

ANDREW. I know. And I wasn't gonna tell you, but then you got so upset about the ... Max settling down thing ...

BECKY. *(Covers her eyes, tears up.)* I'm sorry. *(Cries/gasps.)* Oh, my God, Andrew. It hurts!

ANDREW. You know what? *(Takes her hands in his.)* Tell me what hurts.

BECKY. I had a gun pointed at me!

ANDREW. So it's the gun ...

BECKY. He was black. And that hurts me! Because I was hurt very badly ... twice. It's why I don't talk to my parents ...

ANDREW. A black man ... hurt you? It's OK. It's OK. Tell me how he hurt you.

BECKY. When I was a freshman at Brown, I met a boy who really liked me. He was black ... And my parents said, you know, it's him or it's us. Choose.

ANDREW. Are you serious?

BECKY. And I couldn't face losing my family. So I ended it with

Stefan and I learned after I let him go, that he had truly loved me and my family didn't. I tried to go backwards. But he wouldn't ... I had kind of a breakdown. I had a scholarship and I lost it.

ANDREW. Shit. I'm sorry.

BECKY. Then ... Last year, I was working at a law firm and I became involved with one of the lawyers who was — is — black. I told him that if I committed to him, I would lose my family, so he had to be very sure he wanted me ...

ANDREW. He wasn't sure ...

BECKY. No, he was. I cut ties with my family. I moved into his house. He has a house ... on the water, in Cranston. I was so happy! Then he changed his mind.

ANDREW. Oh, shit.

BECKY. I've been having these terrible racist feelings since the hold-up. I've been thinking that black men have ruined my life and I ... I can't say it.

ANDREW. Say it. Say anything. I told you my blood-on-the-snow thing. Come on ...

BECKY. Walking to the bus, I get pictures in my mind of black men ... being tortured ... God, I fucking hate myself!

ANDREW. Becky, you had a trauma. You're allowed to feel some crazy shit for a while. And you're not gonna act on these thoughts, right? You're small, but you're intense ...

BECKY. Don't say I'm intense! Jason said that when he left me.

ANDREW. It's not a bad thing.

BECKY. Yes, it is. Men don't want intense women.

ANDREW. Uh ... Yeah, we do.

BECKY. You think you do, but you don't. Jason left me. You're fighting with Suzanna ...

ANDREW. We'll get past it. Look. Intensity is a good thing. It means you can love. It's just a matter of, you know, how you channel it.

BECKY. I can see where Suzanna might lash out and that would be so much healthier ...

ANDREW. Healthier for her, maybe.

BECKY. Sometimes the fantasy isn't enough and I think about cutting myself with a knife.

ANDREW. *(Rallying.)* Then we need to go to the hospital. Tonight.

BECKY. I don't have insurance.

ANDREW. I don't care. If you want to hurt yourself, I have to protect you.

BECKY. I feel that. I feel safe with you. It's wonderful. To feel safe. *(This is starting to feel a little … intimate.)*
ANDREW. Do you have any girlfriends? Maybe you could call …
BECKY. I lost them when I moved in with Jason.
ANDREW. Wow. Your friends were all racists?
BECKY. They weren't racist at all, actually. It's just … Jason made me happy and happiness made me mean. To women. Not to Jason.
ANDREW. What did you do?
BECKY. Dumped them. You know the all-female table in the bar? Women drinking fucking Midori sours pretending to like each other while they scan for men.
ANDREW. God, I can't stand women like that …
BECKY. But I am women like that! I got a boyfriend and I dumped all my friends! *(Surveying the room.)* Maybe this is my punishment, you know?
ANDREW. The hold-up?
BECKY. No. This. Back to the studio apartment and the secretary table at happy hour. *(After a beat.)* If not for the hold-up, Andrew … I think Max and I … I think it could have worked.
ANDREW. No —
BECKY. You're an honest person. When you told me Max was coarse on the outside and rich inside … Andrew, I saw that in him!
ANDREW. No. Becky … Forget that. Forget him.
BECKY. Andrew, we slept together.
ANDREW. You … So he did call you.
BECKY. No. I'm so embarrassed. We slept together that night.
ANDREW. After the … robbery?
BECKY. After the police station. We wanted a drink to calm down, but nothing was open. So we went to his hotel.
ANDREW. You went to Boston?
BECKY. No. He had rented a room here for the night.
ANDREW. He rented a room in advance? Are you kidding me?
BECKY. We had some drinks and … It turned kind of bad.
ANDREW. Did he hurt you?
BECKY. Not … sexually. He just wouldn't let me stay overnight.
ANDREW. He what?
BECKY. He gave me cab fare …
ANDREW. Cab fare?
BECKY. I told him I didn't want to be alone after what had happened and he offered me his credit card to get my own room in the hotel.

ANDREW. Let me get this straight. He fucked you —
BECKY. Please don't say that.
ANDREW. He had sex with you, he kicked you out of his bed, and he offered you money.
BECKY. Not for sex! For a hotel or a cab. In his way, he was taking care of me.
ANDREW. No. Becky, he's sick! Listen: I will take care of you. You are never to contact him again. Do you hear me?
BECKY. Yes. I hear you. Yes.

Scene 4

Max and Suzanna in Max's hotel room in Boston. The following night: Wednesday.

SUZANNA. You shouldn't have slept with her, Max.
MAX. She initiated it!
SUZANNA. I don't care. You knew you didn't want to see her again and she'd just been held up with a gun ...
MAX. She initiated it!
SUZANNA. I don't care. It was selfish and sleazy.
MAX. She grabbed me like this. *(He demonstrates on Suzanna.)* She said, "I need this."
SUZANNA. You kicked her out of bed afterwards!
MAX. Oh, come on. I didn't stay in your bed after we ... did it. I have a sleep disorder!
SUZANNA. No, Max. You have an intimacy issue that you pay a doctor to call a sleep disorder.
MAX. Are you a doctor? Have you seen my sleep study?
SUZANNA. Fuck your sleep study. Having sex and then leaving ... or kicking out ... It's degrading. You need to get some sleeping pills.
MAX. You think I haven't tried that? They give me a hangover.
SUZANNA. Love, Max, is worth a hangover.
MAX. Do you understand the pressure of my job? I'm not a ... a barista ... poet ... secretary-boy like Andrew. I control people's money. I can't be off my game!

50

SUZANNA. So your clients matter and your women don't?

MAX. Uhhh ... If you're asking me will I jeopardize people's life savings because women need to cuddle, the answer is no.

SUZANNA. *(After a beat.)* Call Becky Shaw. Call her now.

MAX. No!

SUZANNA. She says she's suicidal, Max. Andrew is afraid to leave her alone. I've barely seen him since this happened.

MAX. That's Andrew's bad, not mine. You pulled that suicidal shit with me, I didn't come running.

SUZANNA. Hence me marrying Andrew and not you. *(A hard silence, then a spike in anger for both.)*

MAX. Say what you want, but give me credit. I cured you. And I did it by refusing to enable the Sylvia Plath, post-collegiate bullshit —

SUZANNA. You cured me? No. Meeting Andrew cured me.

MAX. Yeah? Well, you met Andrew because I kicked your ass. I kicked your ass out of bed and onto that fucking ski trip! *(A beat. He's right.)*

SUZANNA. And I am so, so grateful. Are you trying to torpedo my marriage? If you are, please stop.

MAX. Jesus, Suzanna. You let a crazy woman into your life. You let her into mine. How have I become the bad guy?

SUZANNA. Because you won't help me! That's what loving someone is, Max. It's doing stuff you don't want to do. It's staying in bed all night. It's listening when you can't help. And right now ... today ... this minute ... It is calling Becky fucking Shaw so I can get my husband back! *(Her level of distress surprises and affects Max. He takes it in and then ... a gentleness to his approach.)*

MAX. OK, calm down. Go back to Providence. I'll call her.

SUZANNA. Thank you, Max. Thank you.

MAX. I'm also gonna give you some advice. Your husband is not the fucking Red Cross. The last time he started consoling a cute, suicidal chick, he married her. He hears, "I want to hurt myself" like a fucking mating call.

SUZANNA. No ...

MAX. Yes ...

SUZANNA. Just make her go away. *(Max genuinely wants to ease Suzanna's pain. But the notion of Suzanna's marriage imploding is undeniably appealing, too.)*

Scene 5

Max and Becky in a cafe. Thursday.

BECKY. I understand your reluctance to see me. What happened to us ... on a first date! It's just so crazy ...

MAX. It ... certainly was.

BECKY. Did Detective Hogan call you, too?

MAX. He may have. I think I told you, I'm opening a Boston office for my company, so ... I have a stack of messages I haven't even looked at. *(Off her expression.)* Your messages ... I did receive. I apologize for not returning them. This is a very busy time.

BECKY. I'm sure.

MAX. But I've ... made time. To talk about ... whatever you need to talk about to put this event behind you.

BECKY. I gather from Andrew you feel it already is ... behind you. The hold-up.

MAX. I do. *(She waits for him to say more. He doesn't.)*

BECKY. It's been ... upsetting for me.

MAX. Of course.

BECKY. No, I want to apologize. I was very pushy ... calling you all the time. I regret that. I really do.

MAX. Apology ... accepted.

BECKY. I'm in the same place you are now. I feel ready to just ... be past it and move on.

MAX. Great.

BECKY. *(Forced lightness.)* Our next date should be like a ... daytime visit to the zoo! I don't know. Something completely not dangerous.

MAX. My feeling about all of this, Becky ... We were interrupted. This thing interrupted the normal dating process. Chalk it up to my personal failing, but I don't feel we can get past that. It's just not gonna work.

BECKY. *(She's really thrown.)* OK ... Wow. You're saying ... If not for the robbery, you'd have wanted to see me again?

MAX. Not exactly that —

BECKY. I wondered if this was the reason you weren't calling me.

If you're embarrassed about how you acted during the hold-up, you shouldn't be.

MAX. Embarrassed?

BECKY. You were scared, so was I. If you're running from me ... My feelings for you are only deepened by that glimpse into your vulnerability.

MAX. Becky, you're not understanding me.

BECKY. And I want to. Max, the detective told me — I'm sure he told you, too — that you shouldn't have led the ... perpetrator to your car ...

MAX. Now, wait —

BECKY. No, hear me out. If you're embarrassed about that, I want you to know ... I think it was the right thing to do. And I was there; the detective wasn't.

MAX. Right —

BECKY. I absolutely understand why you feel the robbery ruined our chance. But it doesn't have to. I'm over it now. I don't need to ever mention it again.

MAX. I didn't say the robbery ruined our chance.

BECKY. Yes, you did.

MAX. OK, yes. I did say that because Suzanna told me to. The truth, Becky is ... I don't think we're a good match —

BECKY. Because the robbery is clouding your feelings —

MAX. I knew before the robbery.

BECKY. Can I ask when?

MAX. At the restaurant.

BECKY. So you slept with me knowing I wasn't your match?

MAX. I'm sorry if I misread your signals.

BECKY. Can you tell me why ... you decided that?

MAX. Oh, for God's sake ...

BECKY. I'm not angry. I just want to know what I did —

MAX. Jesus, I'm allowed to not be interested. I don't owe you an explanation.

BECKY. I just want to know what it is about me, so I can — in the future — correct it.

MAX. This! I didn't return your calls. Any normal person would have —

BECKY. But you said you knew at the restaurant. What did I do?

MAX. This! You force people to hurt you.

BECKY. I made you feel you'd hurt me? That's it? You don't want

53

to be with a woman you feel you hurt?

MAX. Would you want to be with a man you could hurt?

BECKY. But that's love, isn't it? Anything that matters carries the potential for hurt …

MAX. Love, Becky. We had one date.

BECKY. I gave you power prematurely. Is that it?

MAX. *(Rising to leave.)* I don't want to do this.

BECKY. This doesn't hurt me! It helps. Please sit for a second. *(And he does.)* I took some wrong turns, Max, and I changed. See, when I was in college …

MAX. I don't … I don't care. *(Recoiling; back-pedaling.)* I'm sorry. This is starting to feel like the second date I didn't want to have.

BECKY. OK. I just wanted you to know that I wasn't always like this. And I feel I can get back to being myself — my good self — if I'm really fearless in examining —

MAX. Great. Do that with a therapist. Not me.

BECKY. OK. Just one last question.

MAX. No.

BECKY. Just as a favor —

MAX. I don't owe you any favors!

BECKY. *(After a beat.)* Then I don't owe you any either. Right?

MAX. Are you threatening me?

BECKY. I'm not good enough to date, but I'm good enough to … to fuck and to be trusted with a confidence that you would not like me to betray. *(Off Max.)* At the police station? I said you have to call Suzanna, she's your family. You said, "She's not family. I don't fuck family." Andrew doesn't know.

MAX. *(Sitting down.)* You're a fraud. *(Max leans across the table and grabs her arm.)*

BECKY. *(Loud enough to be heard.)* Stop it! You're hurting me.

MAX. You care, you understand … as long as you get what you want. You just went from trying to date me to blackmailing me in about three minutes. You're a scary person, Becky, and I knew it the minute I met you.

BECKY. Then you shouldn't have fucked me. *(To Max, quieter.)* If I was that person you just described … I'd have screamed by now and had you arrested for assault. Let go of my arm … and walk away. *(Max lets go of Becky and stands up. He takes a moment to really look at her before he walks out. Becky sits, recovers. She thinks about what Max said about her and her choice to end the encounter without making a scene.)*

Scene 6

Andrew and Suzanna in their apartment. The same day: Thursday.

SUZANNA. Max assaulted her? In a café full of people? I don't believe that.

ANDREW. Assault is my word, but any time a man raises his hand against a woman —

SUZANNA. Assault is your word? What's Becky's word?

ANDREW. He grasped her forearm, Suzanna.

SUZANNA. He grasped her forearm. You left work … You made me leave work … because Max grasped her forearm?

ANDREW. It is never acceptable for a man to dominate a woman by force!

SUZANNA. Agreed. But you said this was an emergency.

ANDREW. This is an emergency, Suzanna!

SUZANNA. No … it isn't. Look, you know I find your radical feminist side an incredible turn-on …

ANDREW. This is not a joke.

SUZANNA. Sweetie, I know that. But I just walked out on a patient who has actual, real problems. In the future … A forearm grab is not an emergency. *(She tries to kiss him. He recoils.)*

ANDREW. Max assaulted my friend, Suzanna. He is out of our lives.

SUZANNA. Out … He's out of yours, maybe.

ANDREW. You want me to be a man and make the decisions in this marriage? I just made one. You, Max — done. *(A beat. Is she gonna escalate this or bullshit agreement and go back to work?)*

SUZANNA. You know what? Fuck you, Andrew. Here's a reality check. What Max is guilty of is fuck-and-run. It's not very nice, but it's also not a war crime. He blew her off. He didn't strangle her cat!

ANDREW. Jesus! Why do you and Max have to use such violent examples to make your points?

SUZANNA. Because we have some fucking perspective on life! Becky needs to get over it and you need to stop the Sir Lancelot bullshit. You have spare time to manufacture drama where none exists …

Put it in your writing so you can get published and we can keep our apartment!

ANDREW. Jesus, I feel like I don't know you.

SUZANNA. Why?

ANDREW. When I met you, Max and your mom were telling you to "get over" your dad's death. I listened and I cared.

SUZANNA. That's true! Your love healed me. But Becky needs to find her own savior, she can't have mine.

ANDREW. She doesn't have anyone else!

SUZANNA. That's not our fault.

ANDREW. Her pain *is* our fault. You knew Max's record with women. Fixing him up with her was thoughtless.

SUZANNA. I have apologized! What more can I do?

ANDREW. You've done enough. It is up to me now to ... *(Off Suzanna's look.)* I'm not going to abandon this woman when she's drowning!

SUZANNA. Right. You'll save her and then you'll abandon her. That's what you do, right? Your anorexic girlfriend gained ten pounds, you married me.

ANDREW. You want to tell yourself I'm turned off by you getting healthy? Go ahead. I'm not turned off by your health, I'm turned off by your character.

SUZANNA. *(Wounded.)* My character?

ANDREW. Max treated Becky like garbage from the moment she walked in that door. And I watched you that night. You didn't care then, and you don't care now. Your lack of compassion for her is incredibly unattractive.

SUZANNA. I do care, Andrew, but ...

ANDREW. But what? How could you fix Max up with her? How could you fix him up with anyone?

SUZANNA. Max is a good man, Andrew. Just because —

ANDREW. *(Overlapping.)* Are you kidding me? Fine. You know what? We've reached an impasse on this Max ... thing. I'm gonna stay with friends for a couple days.

SUZANNA. Why?

ANDREW. I need to think.

SUZANNA. Think about ... us? Oh, no. No. Andrew, listen to me. When I married you, I married up. I married a better person than I am. I love that you want to help Becky. I love that you don't think the bubbla story is funny and I love that pornography makes you cry.

You're good like my dad was good —
ANDREW. Your dad was a dishonest, irresponsible alcoholic. Jesus, Suzanna. Your dad was good ... Max is good ... Here's a "reality check" for you: Loving Suzanna is not the sole criteria for goodness! *(Andrew starts for the bedroom to pack some stuff and leave ...)*
SUZANNA. *(To stop him.)* Wait. Andrew, I'm gonna tell you something. Max doesn't know and you can never tell him ... My father bought Max. From his father.
ANDREW. What do you mean, he bought him?
SUZANNA. He gave Max's dad a lot of money not to send him away. When Max's mom died. His dad was gonna send him to some great-aunt in Texas. And my father said no! He knew it would kill Max, it would break his heart. So he ... He bought him. *(A beat.)* My father was good like you, see? Max wasn't his problem, but he just couldn't walk away. Like you and Becky. It's goodness. You don't have ... feelings for her. Do you? *(A hideous pause.)* Oh, no.
ANDREW. Our problem is not Becky. *(Off her devastation.)* Let's talk in a few days. I think it would be good for you to do some thinking, too.

Scene 7

The living room of Susan Slater's home in Richmond, Virginia. Saturday. Suzanna, alone, with two big duffel bags, checking her cell phone for messages. Max enters.

MAX. Your mother is sleeping. We should get our story straight before she wakes up.
SUZANNA. I'm gonna tell her the truth. Andrew and I fixed you up with a woman and you made her attempt suicide.
MAX. Oh, no —
SUZANNA. Yes! That is why my husband isn't here with me now.
MAX. First of all, she did not attempt suicide. She cut herself. If it were serious, she'd be hospitalized, but she isn't. She's home convalescing with your husband. *(A beat.)* He should be here. This shit you're about to face ... This is way more serious than a cut on the arm.

57

SUZANNA. If you can't get Lester out of jail before Monday, my mom's gonna freak out.

MAX. She should freak out. Lester could go to prison, Suzanna. If he was doing what they say ... It's mail fraud. That's big.

SUZANNA. Not as big as cutting yourself. Apparently.

MAX. That's life and you know it. Two kinds of trouble in life ...

SUZANNA. I don't want the "two kinds of trouble" speech right now.

MAX. Yeah, but you need it. Two kinds of trouble. Sexy and not sexy. Your mother's chronic, degenerative illness? Not sexy. Pretty girl with knife? Sexy. People like me show up when the trouble's not sexy. Indie-rock writer boys —

SUZANNA. I thought crime and jail were in the "sexy" category.

MAX. Not when it's mail fraud. If Lester had shot somebody, your husband would be here now.

SUZANNA. Are you sure what Becky did isn't serious?

MAX. She cut her arm! It's teenager shit. You remember what I told you when you wanted to do it.

SUZANNA. Yes.

MAX. You're too old for it. Cutting yourself over the age of eighteen is just embarrassing. Everyone at the ER will laugh at you.

SUZANNA. You're harsh, Max.

MAX. It worked. You never did it, did you?

SUZANNA. No. I didn't. *(Susan enters. She just woke up.)* Hi, Mama. Did we wake you?

SUSAN. *(Overlapping.)* Yes, you did. Where's Andrew?

SUZANNA. *(Lousy liar under pressure.)* Andrew has a coworker who tried to ... She ... you know ... suicide. He's helping her.

SUSAN. *(After a beat.)* He's had an affair and you've separated. I'm sorry.

SUZANNA. No! Jesus, Mom!

SUSAN. Max, what is our plan? Lester needs a very good lawyer and, obviously, I don't know anyone.

SUZANNA. Are we allowed to talk about, you know, what he did?

SUSAN. He didn't do anything. Now I'd like to hear the plan. *(A beat. There's no budging her.)*

MAX. I have three names ... of lawyers with expertise in this area —

SUSAN. Have you called them?

MAX. It's Saturday. I only have office numbers.

SUSAN. Use your Lexis-Nexis account. Get their home numbers.

MAX. OK. Fine. *(Max leaves to use Susan's computer, leaving mother and daughter alone. After some silence …)*

SUSAN. Don't let your pride cloud your judgment.

SUZANNA. Excuse me?

SUSAN. If you need money to leave your husband, ask Max for a loan —

SUZANNA. I'm not leaving my husband!

SUSAN. No one respects a woman who forgives infidelity. It kept Hillary Clinton from becoming president.

SUZANNA. Andrew is not cheating on me. We fixed one of his coworkers up with Max and the date went badly, she freaked out.

SUSAN. Did Max rape her?

SUZANNA. Of course, he didn't rape her! Are you insane?

SUSAN. Why does someone attempt suicide after a bad date?

SUZANNA. Forget it. The point is, Andrew has the decency to face the problem, Max doesn't.

SUSAN. Well, that's very gallant of Andrew. It's a good thing Max was available to take care of us.

SUZANNA. I don't want to talk about this. *(A beat.)* Wait a second. You're telling me that one sexual indiscretion merits divorce, but you allowed —

SUSAN. *(Whispering close.)* Listen to me. This business about your father being a homosexual … It's absurd. It's Max fabricating in order to dominate and control.

SUZANNA. Whoa. That's not at all where I was going …

SUSAN. I'm sorry. Go on.

SUZANNA. I just … You tell me to divorce Andrew over an affair, but you let Lester lie and get arrested. Why do I have to play by different rules than you?

SUSAN. Well, I don't have your assets, now do I? A relationship is a deal between equals. It's a mutually advantageous bargain —

SUZANNA. Oh, my God. Did you teach Max that?

SUSAN. I'm sick. Money is my only asset.

SUZANNA. You don't really believe that.

MAX. *(Returning.)* Well, I just got screamed at for interrupting dinner. But we have a lawyer.

SUSAN. Max, thank God for you. You never fail me.

MAX. I'm gonna go meet him, bring him up to speed. You ladies want to come? *(The women grumble "no's" in unison.)* Of course you don't. *(A beat. He's uncomfortable leaving them alone together.)* So …

I'll be back. *(Max leaves. A beat. Suzanna goes to the window and watches him get in his car.)*

SUZANNA. Mom, that stuff about Dad ... It has really messed with my head. *(Susan swats the air dismissively.)* Why are you giving me the exasperation look?

SUSAN. Please. I love Max like a son, but he's a powermonger and a liar.

SUZANNA. Max made it up? Dad wasn't gay?

SUSAN. The important point is this: Since you were very young, Max has lied and manipulated to foster your dependence.

SUZANNA. Max doesn't manipulate me.

SUSAN. Suzanna, don't be dense.

SUZANNA. Not when we were kids ...

SUSAN. Please. When Max moved in with us, he knew he was not to watch horror movies. More importantly, he knew you couldn't handle those movies. All those nights we let you two sleep in the den in your sleeping bags? He orchestrated that! He showed you those vile, horrible movies until you were afraid to sleep alone.

SUZANNA. No. Max loves me.

SUSAN. Exactly. That's why he hobbled you so you couldn't stray.

SUZANNA. If you saw Max trying to hobble me, why didn't you stop him?

SUSAN. We knew you could never take care of yourself. We saw in Max's devotion a kind of security.

SUZANNA. OK. Wow. So ... Max telling me Dad was gay, this was a lie to "hobble" me?

SUSAN. Probably. Yoshi had a strange adoration for your father. It's possible he made some overture. Whether or not your father had reciprocal feelings ... I have no idea.

SUZANNA. No idea? You were married to him!

SUSAN. We're a different generation, Suzanna ...

SUZANNA. Meaning ...

SUSAN. Meaning your father and I allowed for pockets of mystery in our marriage and I would advise you to do the same.

SUZANNA. "Pocket of mystery" sounds like code for gay.

SUSAN. Was he gay? Perhaps. Did he have affairs with men? No. Your father was deeply moral and would never have broken his vows. Also, he was not a sexual person.

SUZANNA. Every human is sexual, Mom.

SUSAN. Not true. Sexuality is like intelligence. We're all born with different endowments. Some people are retarded and they eat paint, others split atoms and write symphonies.

SUZANNA. Oh, my God …

SUSAN. I'm sorry, Suzanna. When Max told me this about your father and Yoshi … It was like someone telling me the Mongoloid who bags my groceries had found the cancer cure. I have to allow for the possibility while remaining exceedingly dubious.

SUZANNA. God, I'm really confused.

SUSAN. He's gone. What does it matter —

SUZANNA. If it's true, it means I didn't really know him. And I thought we were so close …

SUSAN. You were very close. There are pockets of privacy within "closeness." That's as it should be. My advice to you … Never mind. You don't want it.

SUZANNA. I do want it.

SUSAN. Your generation is fixated on "intimacy." That's why your marriages don't last. You think marriage and family require absolute honesty. They do not.

SUZANNA. Can you truly know someone when they're lying to you?

SUSAN. Why do you have to truly know them? Why?

SUZANNA. Because that's … love?

SUSAN. It's a prescription for misery. It's like those television commercials where they take a microscope into your kitchen and show you a lot of germs the naked eye can't see. It's stupid. If you look hard enough at anything … *anyone,* you will be revolted by what you see.

SUZANNA. You think if you'd known Dad, you would have been revolted by him?

SUSAN. *(After a beat.)* By his weakness. Yes. If you're gay, be gay. Have some guts. *(After a beat.)* Now, you will never hear me buy into any of this new-age nonsense about my illness being a gift. It has ruined my life and I hate it. But. It was a gift to me in this one respect. It meant I couldn't leave my marriage.

SUZANNA. If you hadn't had MS, would you have left?

SUSAN. I would have felt I could do better than your father. And I would have been wrong.

SUZANNA. *(A beat; hard to say.)* I think I'm revolted by Max. But if I were to lose him … I'm afraid I wouldn't survive. How is that possible? I can't live without him, but I don't want him.

SUSAN. The heart wants what the heart wants. I want Lester with a ferocity you can't imagine. I see his flaws ...

SUZANNA. Max isn't good, Mom. Max isn't good and Andrew is.

SUSAN. Be careful chasing after goodness. Goodness and incompetence too often go hand-in-hand in men. Your father's financial irresponsibility ... It's unforgivable really.

SUZANNA. Andrew's not incompetent.

SUSAN. He scribbles and brews coffee. If he's not going to pull his weight financially, he must love and care for you in spades to compensate —

SUZANNA. He does.

SUSAN. He isn't here, Suzanna! And Max is. What would you have done, if not for Max? What would I have done?

SUZANNA. I would have driven down here and ... handled this.

SUSAN. You wouldn't have done a good job.

SUZANNA. I think that's awful for a mother to say.

SUSAN. It's the truth. There's power in knowing where you stand.

SUZANNA. Mom —

SUSAN. I told Max he had to get rich if he wanted women to swoon. And you see? He followed my advice.

SUZANNA. Well done, Mom! He's an emotional cripple! *(The doorbell rings.)* Do not tell him we talked about this. *(Suzanna opens the door, expecting Max. It's Andrew and Becky — though the audience doesn't yet see Becky.)*

ANDREW. I promised at the hospital I'd take care of her, but I wanted to be here. *(Andrew steps into the house.)* Hey ... Susan. I'm sorry about Lester. This is my friend, Becky ... *(Becky, cautious and sheepish, now enters. She has a bandage on one forearm.)*

BECKY. Andrew is helping me. I hope it's OK he brought me ...

SUSAN. Well, you're here now, OK or not. Come in. *(Andrew and Becky step fully inside.)*

ANDREW. Where's Max?

SUSAN. Max is meeting with our lawyer. He has the situation in hand. I'm very relieved.

ANDREW. That's great. *(A terribly awkward silence.)*

SUSAN. *(To Becky.)* What did you do to your arm?

BECKY. Oh! This? I cut it. *(More awkward silence.)* I should actually maybe change the bandage ...

SUSAN. I'll show you the bathroom ... *(Susan starts to lead Becky out. Becky looks to Andrew to follow.)*

ANDREW. Maybe I should ... I was at the hospital, so —

SUSAN. I raised two children, Andrew. I can supervise changing a Band-Aid. Come on. *(Becky looks afraid, but Andrew doesn't intervene. Susan and Becky leave the room. A beat and ...)*
ANDREW. I had no choice, Suzanna. She has no health insurance! The only way they'd let her leave was if I promised to be responsible — *(Suzanna kisses him suddenly and forcefully.)*
SUZANNA. I'm so glad you're here!
ANDREW. Of course I'm here. Are you freaking out?
SUZANNA. About Lester?
ANDREW. About your dad. It's the anniversary.
SUZANNA. You ... You remembered. Andrew, I don't want to lose you to Becky. I can be a better person. I want to be ...
ANDREW. I don't want to be with Becky.
SUZANNA. You don't? Really?
ANDREW. No. But I think I led her on and I'm afraid she'll do something if I walk away.
SUZANNA. Did you sleep with her?
ANDREW. No! I wouldn't do that.
SUZANNA. But you wanted to. *(Before he can answer.)* No, don't answer that.
ANDREW. I can do better, too. What you said about me ... that I save women and then abandon them ... I don't want to be that guy. I want this marriage. *(A beat. Suzanna wants to probe, to autopsy his answer, but thinks better of it.)*
SUZANNA. Good enough for me. What should we do about Becky?
ANDREW. I don't know. The whole ride down here, I'm thinking ... And I have no idea.
SUZANNA. Ten hours of thinking and you have no idea? Do you have human waste in your cranium where a brain should be?
ANDREW. Suzanna ... I will get back in that car ...
SUZANNA. Don't! I'm sorry. I can do this. I can be the ... decider. *(After a beat.)* We'll get Becky another therapist and we'll loan her ... Fuck. We'll give her the money. We can see her together, but you can't be with her alone outside of work. I think to make this marriage work we have to be in it full-time, you know?
ANDREW. I think that's fair. I think the same should apply to you and Max.
SUZANNA. That's totally different. Just because you don't like

him …

ANDREW. It's more than that. Stop pulling this "he's my brother" crap. I know there's more there.

SUZANNA. There isn't more there.

ANDREW. That's a lie, Suzanna. You want to make this marriage work? The two of you need to … stop.

SUZANNA. Can I still have my phone time?

ANDREW. I wish you didn't need it, but … I guess so. OK.

SUZANNA. But I can't see him anymore.

ANDREW. I think … Same rules for you as for me. You can see Max with me. *(As she takes that in …)* I better go check on Becky. This agreement? We should tell them today. *(Andrew goes to find/rescue Becky. Suzanna sits, thinks. Max returns …)*

MAX. What the fuck is going on?

SUZANNA. Were you … watching the house?

MAX. Did he bring her here? I'll kill him …

SUZANNA. He had to bring her; she's on suicide watch.

MAX. Get her out of here. Now.

SUZANNA. Don't give me orders, Max!

MAX. I'm here taking care of your mother! I'm spending time I do not have —

SUZANNA. You can leave. I can handle it. You got the lawyer, Andrew is here. You can go.

MAX. No. I used my good name to get us a lawyer. I'm not gonna turn him over to your indie-rock boy-toy.

SUZANNA. He's my husband, Max. *(After a beat.)* And that is … permanent.

MAX. Why are you looking at me like you're breaking up with me?

SUZANNA. Max, stuff is gonna have to change with us.

MAX. What "stuff"?

SUZANNA. Andrew and I just made an agreement. He can't be alone with Becky, and I can't be alone with you …

MAX. What?!

SUZANNA. It's not appropriate for us to be emotionally intimate when I'm married to Andrew.

MAX. Emotionally intimate? According to you, I'm not capable of that.

SUZANNA. We can talk on the phone, but … we can't be alone, it just gets too blurry.

MAX. This is because of Becky.

SUZANNA. Not entirely —

MAX. It is. God, I fucking hate that woman. She's a nutcase, so our relationship has to change?

SUZANNA. Yes.

MAX. How? How does a twenty-five-year friendship change because of her?

SUZANNA. Up until this … I had doubts. I thought maybe we should be together. But now I don't have them. Doubts.

MAX. If you have don't have doubts, then why are we blurry? *(Off her silence.)* I'll rephrase the question. What are your "doubts" about me?

SUZANNA. *(Careful.)* You have always had the ability to tune out other people's pain when it inconveniences you.

MAX. Excuse me?

SUZANNA. Not mine. You have always been there for me and for my parents. I'm talking about other people … Iraq is not your problem, Becky is not your problem …

MAX. That's right. They're not. And I make no apologies. Unless you're Gandhi or Jesus, you have a limited sphere of responsibility. You have a plot of land and the definition of a moral life is tending that plot of land —

SUZANNA. You need new material. I've heard the "plot of land" speech.

MAX. Becky Shaw is not on my plot of land! You are. And I tend my plot. I will always tend my plot.

SUZANNA. You make me sound like an obligation. Am I more than that to you?

MAX. Yes! If I didn't want you on my plot, I would rip you out and compost you. I want you on my plot. *(After a beat.)* Bring Becky in here and I'll apologize. We'll put this behind us.

SUZANNA. It's not that simple.

MAX. I will apologize! I will pay her damages, whatever you need. I want her erased from our lives.

SUZANNA. This is exactly what I'm talking about, Max! You erase people. That's wrong.

MAX. Give me another example. Aside from the war and Becky, how do I "erase" people?

SUZANNA. You watch pornography.

MAX. What? You watch it, too!

SUZANNA. But I feel guilty when I watch it! You don't.

MAX. Are you fucking kidding me? I'm gonna lose you because I don't feel guilty when I watch porn?

SUZANNA. Pornography makes Andrew cry.

MAX. That is the stupidest thing I've ever heard.

SUZANNA. I don't think it is.

MAX. Does pornography make you cry?

SUZANNA. No, but it should and I wish it did.

MAX. This is completely insane. You cannot tell me — *(Andrew enters on top of this ...)*

ANDREW. Susan really wants to go to Lester's visiting hour, so ... Hi, Max.

SUZANNA. OK. Can you just give us one —

ANDREW. Oh, sure. Sure. *(He leaves the room. This is politeness, yes, but it's the politeness of a man who knows he's won.)*

SUZANNA. *(To Max.)* Why don't you go back to Boston, and we'll talk in a few days.

MAX. I can't. I'm busy.

SUZANNA. Max —

MAX. I have a very full schedule between ... laughing at rape videos and sneering at the troops.

SUZANNA. That isn't fair.

MAX. No. This. This. Isn't fair. Anything else you want to say, you better say now. *(He could cut her off and she knows it. The time is now if there's anything left to say.)*

SUZANNA. Today is Saturday, right? It's the third?

MAX. *(Totally perplexed, but he checks his cell phone ...)* I don't fuck-ing ... Yeah, it's the third. You need anything else before you wash your hands of me? You want the weather? Stock quotes? Horoscope?

SUZANNA. I don't want to wash my hands of you.

MAX. You just did. *(Susan enters, Becky and Andrew trail cautiously behind her.)*

SUSAN. I want to go to the prison and I want to go now.

MAX. It's not a prison, Susan. It's a jail.

SUSAN. You can call it whatever you like if you drive me there.

SUZANNA. OK. Everybody listen up. Max feels he needs to stay here because he initiated contact with the attorney. Andrew and Becky and I are going back to Providence.

SUSAN. You have a responsibility here.

SUZANNA. I'm aware of that, but Andrew and I have set some new boundaries for our marriage and ... He's not allowed to spend ten hours in a car alone with Becky.

BECKY. I feel like I've caused so much trouble for you and I just wanted to —

SUZANNA. *(Overlapping.)* You have, actually. So that's it. Let's go. *(Becky starts to weep, sits down ...)*

ANDREW. Becky ...

BECKY. I can't. I'm sorry. I'll take the train.

ANDREW. When we get back to Providence ... Susie and I are gonna help you.

BECKY. This is incredibly painful for me. To get back in that car ... with the two of you ...

ANDREW. You're right. I think the train is a great idea ... Susie?

SUZANNA. Look into it.

MAX. *(Leaving.)* I'll do that. *(Horrible, awkward waiting.)*

ANDREW. You're gonna be OK ...

SUSAN. Becky and I had a conversation. She knows what needs to be done.

SUZANNA. I'd like to screen any recommendations my mother —

BECKY. No, it was good advice. I need to get back in school, I do.

SUSAN. The story about the black boyfriends and the racist parents. Write that up and re-apply to Brown. You'll get in. *(After a beat.)* You may have been very victimized in your life; you may be a complete con artist. I don't know. My sense is you fall somewhere in the middle. Truth or con ... It's unattractive. We pity Job; we do not fall in love with him.

SUZANNA. Mom, don't.

BECKY. It's OK. I'm not afraid of the truth.

SUSAN. *(To Becky.)* Learn to lie. When someone with damage — as we have damage — courts a lover, we must be like the pedophile with the candy. Lure with candy no matter how frightful your nature and your intent.

BECKY. You're right. You're absolutely right.

SUSAN. You're a beautiful woman; the only thing broken about you is your timing.

BECKY. I had a chance with Max, didn't I?

SUSAN. We don't look back. We look forward.

MAX. *(Returning.)* She won't make the six o'clock and the next one's four A.M.

BECKY. I don't mind waiting. I could help ... I could make sandwiches for you to take to Lester.

SUSAN. I think that's a wonderful idea.

BECKY. Max, what would you like —
MAX. I would like you to try harder the next time you attempt suicide. That is what I would like.
SUSAN. Max!
SUZANNA. OK. Becky, comes with us. We'll buy a book on tape. Let's go. *(Becky, resigned, stands up. The threesome move towards leaving.)*
ANDREW. OK ... Susan, I hope things work out OK with Lester. And I just wanted to acknowledge ... today.
SUSAN. Acknowledge today?
ANDREW. The anniversary of Richard's death. I know it's really hard ... *(Suzanna looks to Max. Whether or not he looks back is up to you.)*
SUSAN. Life is hard, Andrew. An anniversary is just a number. *(Andrew leads Becky out.)*
SUZANNA. Mama, you're in good hands.
SUSAN. I know. *(Suzanna looks at Max, then leaves.)* This is a very impractical solution, you know. If Lester isn't released Monday and you can't stay —
MAX. I'll hire someone for you. Don't worry about that. *(A beat; an edge.)* It's time for you to sell the house. I want to see you put that in motion before I leave.
SUSAN. Fine. We'll discuss it after we visit Lester. I'll comb my hair and we'll go. I'll buy you a wonderful dinner.
MAX. And ... I know this game. You don't talk about money over dinner.
SUSAN. That's right. I don't. *(Susan leaves the room. Max stews for a couple of beats ... Angry and hurt, he'd like to force the issue about the house. But he won't. Becky returns.)*
BECKY. I'm taking the four A.M. train ...
MAX. No —
BECKY. They're gone.
MAX. We're going out. You can't —
BECKY. I'll just wait here. Until it's time. *(Stand-off. Max is dangerously angry. Becky sits down, settles in.)* We've lost them, you know. Suzanna and Andrew ...
MAX. Don't.
BECKY. And what I came back to say ... Max, we'll be fine without them.
MAX. There is no "we," Becky —

BECKY. I know your father abandoned you. My parents abandoned me, too!

MAX. *(In her face, stifling fury.)* My father did not abandon me.

BECKY. *(A rush to get this out before he stops her.)* Listen to me, Max. We have damage. People like Andrew and Suzanna will always run from us when we show them who we are. *(Aim and ... fire:)* I see everything you are and I'm still here. *(A beat.)* When I was at the hospital, they asked me for a name ... someone they should call in an emergency. A spouse, a parent, a child. I don't have any of those people. You don't either. *(Susan returns, surprised to see Becky.)*

SUSAN. You're still here ...

MAX. We're dropping her at the train station.

SUSAN. I thought the next train was four A.M.

MAX. We're dropping her at the train! This is fucking over! This is the end of it.

SUSAN. *(Snapping back.)* Max! You are and ever will be a guest in my home. Adjust your tone. *(Composed now.)* Becky will stay with us until it's time for her train. *(To Becky.)* My boyfriend is unjustly incarcerated. That is as much stress as I will tolerate today. If you're going to be disturbed by visiting a prison, stay here.

BECKY. Oh, don't worry. Life is disturbing, right? It's just a prison.

SUSAN. Nicely put. I'm going to buy you both a wonderful dinner and some really excellent wine. We'll have a nice evening and put all of this behind us. But first we have to go to prison. *(Susan leaves the house, confident Max and Becky will follow. And they will. But first, they size each other up. Suzanna and Andrew are gone, it's true. What are the possibilities? Becky takes a step towards Max. When he doesn't flinch or pounce, she takes another.)*

End of Play

PROPERTY LIST

TV remote
Cell phone
Laptop
Wine, glasses
Bag with bottle of wine
Cell phones
Coffee or food
Beer and pizza
2 duffel bags

SOUND EFFECTS

True-crime TV program
Horror movie
Phone rings
Doorbell buzzer
Doorbell

NEW PLAYS

★ **CLYBOURNE PARK by Bruce Norris.** WINNER OF THE 2011 PULITZER PRIZE AND 2012 TONY AWARD. Act One takes place in 1959 as community leaders try to stop the sale of a home to a black family. Act Two is set in the same house in the present day as the now predominantly African-American neighborhood battles to hold its ground. "Vital, sharp-witted and ferociously smart." –NY Times. "A theatrical treasure…Indisputably, uproariously funny." –Entertainment Weekly. [4M, 3W] ISBN: 978-0-8222-2697-0

★ **WATER BY THE SPOONFUL by Quiara Alegría Hudes.** WINNER OF THE 2012 PULITZER PRIZE. A Puerto Rican veteran is surrounded by the North Philadelphia demons he tried to escape in the service. "This is a very funny, warm, and yes uplifting play." –Hartford Courant. "The play is a combination poem, prayer and app on how to cope in an age of uncertainty, speed and chaos." –Variety. [4M, 3W] ISBN: 978-0-8222-2716-8

★ **RED by John Logan.** WINNER OF THE 2010 TONY AWARD. Mark Rothko has just landed the biggest commission in the history of modern art. But when his young assistant, Ken, gains the confidence to challenge him, Rothko faces the agonizing possibility that his crowning achievement could also become his undoing. "Intense and exciting." –NY Times. "Smart, eloquent entertainment." –New Yorker. [2M] ISBN: 978-0-8222-2483-9

★ **VENUS IN FUR by David Ives.** Thomas, a beleaguered playwright/director, is desperate to find an actress to play Vanda, the female lead in his adaptation of the classic sadomasochistic tale Venus in Fur. "Ninety minutes of good, kinky fun." –NY Times. "A fast-paced journey into one man's entrapment by a clever, vengeful female." –Associated Press. [1M, 1W] ISBN: 978-0-8222-2603-1

★ **OTHER DESERT CITIES by Jon Robin Baitz.** Brooke returns home to Palm Springs after a six-year absence and announces that she is about to publish a memoir dredging up a pivotal and tragic event in the family's history—a wound they don't want reopened. "Leaves you feeling both moved and gratifyingly sated." –NY Times. "A genuine pleasure." –NY Post. [2M, 3W] ISBN: 978-0-8222-2605-5

★ **TRIBES by Nina Raine.** Billy was born deaf into a hearing family and adapts brilliantly to his family's unconventional ways, but it's not until he meets Sylvia, a young woman on the brink of deafness, that he finally understands what it means to be understood. "A smart, lively play." –NY Times. "[A] bright and boldly provocative drama." –Associated Press. [3M, 2W] ISBN: 978-0-8222-2751-9

DRAMATISTS PLAY SERVICE, INC.
440 Park Avenue South, New York, NY 10016 212-683-8960 Fax 212-213-1539
postmaster@dramatists.com www.dramatists.com